THE COMPLETE STAGE
PLANNING KIT
Gill Davies

A & C BLACK ■ LONDON

1405562 7

Introduction

The Complete Stage Planning Kit

This provides all the paper matter needed to organise a theatrical production. It includes forms, checklists and notes for each unit of the production team, including the director, set designer, props, wardrobe, make-up, stage manager and publicity – every department, in fact!

The Kit consists of a wide range of charts, checklists and forms, each one designed to save valuable time and help theatre companies achieve a smooth production.

All the pages are pre-punched and ready to file. Samples of completed forms and general advice can be found at the end of every section.

The relevant pages can be taken out and given to each department's section. Those forms that need to be photocopied for several departments are gathered together in the final section of the book.

All the pages in this book are cleared of photocopying restrictions. Moreover, the Kit comes complete with a CD from which all the forms can be reproduced.

Using the CD

All the pages of the book are reproduced on the CD. Simply choose the pages or sections you wish to reproduce and print these. The layout and information cannot be edited on disc.

Contents

First published 2003 by

A & C Black (Publishers) Limited

Alderman House, 37 Soho Square

London W1D 3QZ

ISBN 0-7136-6585-8

© Playne Books Limited 2003

CIP catalogue records for this book are available from the British Library and the Library of Congress.

All rights reserved. While the forms within the book and on the CD are cleared of copyright and may be reproduced, it is not permissible to copy the CD.

While every effort has been made to trace copyright holders and seek permission to use material, to give credit for this, and to verify facts and information, the publishers cannot be held responsible for any inadvertent errors or omissions. If informed of these, they would be glad to rectify any future edition of the book.

While great care has been taken to verify facts and methods described in this book, neither the publisher nor the author can accept liability for any loss, damage or injury, howsoever caused.

The Complete Stage Planning Kit

was conceived, edited and designed by

Playne Books Limited

Chapel House

Trefin, Haverfordwest

Pembrokeshire SA62 5AU

United Kingdom

Author

© Gill Davies 2003

Editor

Vivienne Kay

Designers and illustrators

Richard Cotton

David Playne

Typeset in Glypha

Printed in Hong Kong

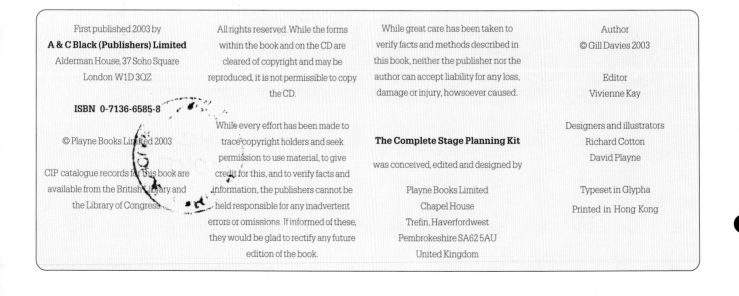

Planning and organisation getting started

Launching a new group

What are the essentials?

Productions by both brand new companies and established theatre groups need:

Careful planning by a committee or equivalent

Someone to direct

People to perform

Backstage help

Front of house personnel

Funding

Advertising

Space to rehearse

A venue for performances

A new drama group can be initiated by word of mouth or advertising within the community – but how many people are required?

A society can be formed by just two or three people, doing a little of everything! The minimum quantity is the number of the cast (doubling up as required), at least one technical body to control lighting and sound, plus the front of house team. Cast members can undertake some pre-performance backstage work while their partners or family may be persuaded to help behind the scenes and front of house during shows.

When choosing a venue, what is important?

1
A suitable stage area

2
Audience seating

3
Lighting equipment or the means to establish this

4
Toilets – for audience and cast

5
Changing room – and somewhere to do make-up

6
Fire exits and signs

Also . . .

7
Are there storage facilities available for costumes, properties and scenery?
If not, what are the alternatives?

8
Are there facilities for catering?

Formalities and committees

What are the essentials?

Whether or not a full committee is formed, the following formalities must be addressed:

1
The group should have a name

2
It needs a postal address

3
It will need a secretary

4
A full committee will require a constitution and various officers. These should include:
Chairman
Secretary
Treasurer

5
An auditor may need to be appointed to oversee all the accounts

6
The group will need a bank account and a cheque book, with agreed signatories

7
The group's name and address should be sent to regional drama organisers and to any other appropriate holders of listings and directories

Planning and organisation people needed   **1**.2

You will need to find suitable people to undertake the following jobs:

Job	Name	Telephone	E-mail
Director/Producer			
Stage manager			
Accounts			
Front of House			
Lighting and Electrics			
Make-up			
Prompt			
Properties			
Publicity			
Secretary			
Set construction			
Set designer			
Set painting			
Sound			
Stage hands			
Ticket selling			
Tickets, posters and programmes			
Wardrobe			
If required			
Box Office			
Fundraisers			
Scriptwriter			
Special Effects			
If catering			
Bar Staff			
Caterers			
Waitresses			
For a musical production			
Choreographer			
Musicians			
Pianist/Accompanist			

Planning and organisation pre-production

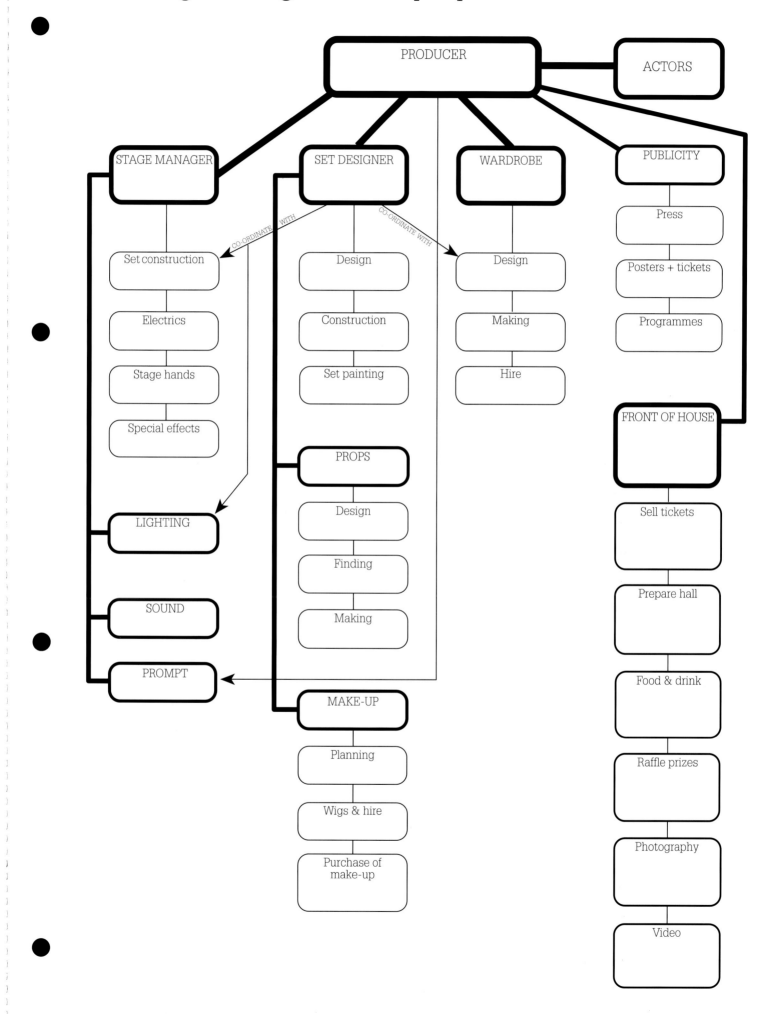

Planning and organisation during production

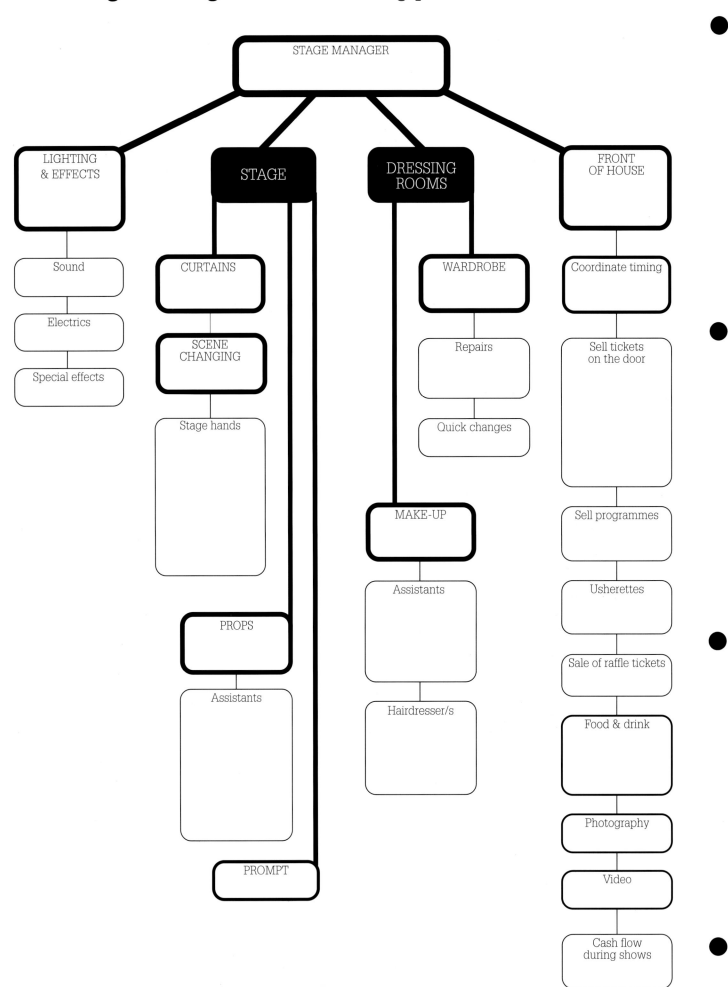

Planning and organisation planning the budget   **1**.5

Production

	1st budget	2nd budget	Actual cost
	Date	Date	Date
Red tape: licences, insurance, copyright clearance and so on			
Scripts and music scores			
Schedules etc: typing and photocopies			
Hire of hall and rehearsal rooms			
Front of house, hire of seating, seting up a box office etc			
Costumes: making and hire			
Make-up and wigs: restocking and hire, tissues and cold cream			
Making the sets: materials, wood, canvas, fabric, paint, nuts and bolts and so on			
Hiring set items			
Lighting and electrics			
Sound			
Special effects			
Properties			
Any prizes or hand-outs to the audience during play			
Publicity: posters, press advertisements, direct mail and any sundry advance information			
Printing: tickets and programmes			
Communications and administration: stamps and telephone calls			
Catering: food, wine, coffees or whatever			
Raffle prizes and tickets			
Miscellaneous production costs, specific to the play			
After-play parties and entertainment			
Flowers (or equivalent) for the after-play presentations			
Contingency allowance			
Total			

Planning and organisation red tape checklist   **1**.6

Task	Who is doing this	Date applied for	Date received
Book venue for performances			
Book venues for rehearsals			
Entertainment licence			
Submit seating plans			
Organise scripts or order play copies			
Sort license to perform play and pay royalties for this			
Check if a video is permissible;clear copyright for this			
Clear copyright for music and recordings			
Check insurance cover			
Check public liability			
Inform fire authorities			
Sort electrics			
Check health regulations if catering			
Organise licence to sell alcohol			

Planning and organisation useful contacts **1**.7

Suppliers	Publicity	Red tape contacts
Costume and wig hire	Local press	Hall committee contacts
Lighting sales and hire		Caretakers/janitors
Sound equipment sales and hire		Script sources and publishers
Set and property hire	Radio stations	
Timber merchants	Television stations	
Paint suppliers	Local newsletter publishers	Performing Rights
DIY shops	Drama news publishers	Issuers of entertainment licences
Professional caterers	Libraries	Issuers of alcohol licences
Make-up suppliers	Schools and colleges	Fire and safety officers
Electrical suppliers		Electricity Board
Printers		Insurance contacts
Graphic designers		Local council
Wine merchants and glass hire companies	Inns, pubs and restaurants	Advisory groups
Taxis and mini-buses		

Planning and organisation audition notification form **1**.12

Society

_____

are now planning a production of

_____

which will be performed on the following dates

_____

_____

_____

_____

_____

_____

_____

_____

_____

We should be glad of your support and would like to invite you to one or more of the auditions on

_____

_____

_____

_____

_____

_____

Please complete the form below and return by

_____

to the following

_____

_____

_____

_____

Telephone

_____

Fax

_____

E-mail

_____

Unless the circumstances are exceptional, only those actors who audition can be considered for a part. However, if you cannot attend on any of these dates, but would like to be involved backstage, please telephone to discuss this with

_____

We should be delighted if any backstage members would like to attend, too. It is a great opportunity to meet up and to find out at an early stage what the production will involve. Also, please do let us know if there is anyone new or a past member you think we should contact this time.

Meanwhile, do return the enclosed form – and we look forward to seeing you soon

Best wishes

- -

Name

_____

Address

_____

_____

_____

_____

_____

_____

Telephone

_____

Fax

_____

E mail

_____

I would like to be considered for a part in

_____

I shall be coming to the audition(s) on

_____

I am especially interested in the following kind of role

❏ straight   ❏ humorous   ❏ singing

I should prefer a

❏ small   ❏ medium   ❏ large role

❏ I should prefer to help backstage

❏ Sorry, I cannot be involved this time

Please tick appropriate box

Planning and organisation photograph order forms **1**.13

Photo order form		
Name		
Telephone		
Film no.	neg no.	quantity
Total quantity		
@		
Total cost		

Photo order form		
Name		
Telephone		
Film no.	neg no.	quantity
Total quantity		
@		
Total cost		

Photo order form		
Name		
Telephone		
Film no.	neg no.	quantity
Total quantity		
@		
Total cost		

Planning and organisation notes for next production **1**.14

Element	Comments	Suggestions
Script		
Auditions and casting		
Line-learning		
Cast reliability		
Rehearsals and schedule		
Sets and stage hands		
Lighting, sound, special effects		
Costumes		
Properties		
Music		
Publicity		
Posters and programmes		
Fund raising and raffle		
Ticket sales		
Stage management		
Venue and seating arrangements		
Audience attendance		
Was the budget workable?		
Front of House and catering		
Photography and video		

From	Date	Show

Planning and organisation new members/patrons 1.15

Name

Telephone

Fax

E-mail

❏ straight role ❏ humorous role ❏ singing role

❏ small role ❏ medium role ❏ large role

❏ stage manager ❏ producer ❏ publicity

❏ stage hand ❏ build/paint sets ❏ make-up

❏ find/make props ❏ costumes ❏ lighting

❏ sound ❏ music/dance ❏ **Patron**

Any previous stage experience?

Name

Telephone

Fax

E-mail

❏ straight role ❏ humorous role ❏ singing role

❏ small role ❏ medium role ❏ large role

❏ stage manager ❏ producer ❏ publicity

❏ stage hand ❏ build/paint sets ❏ make-up

❏ find/make props ❏ costumes ❏ lighting

❏ sound ❏ music/dance ❏ **Patron**

Any previous stage experience?

Name

Telephone

Fax

E-mail

❏ straight role ❏ humorous role ❏ singing role

❏ small role ❏ medium role ❏ large role

❏ stage manager ❏ producer ❏ publicity

❏ stage hand ❏ build/paint sets ❏ make-up

❏ find/make props ❏ costumes ❏ lighting

❏ sound ❏ music/dance ❏ **Patron**

Any previous stage experience?

Name

Telephone

Fax

E-mail

❏ straight role ❏ humorous role ❏ singing role

❏ small role ❏ medium role ❏ large role

❏ stage manager ❏ producer ❏ publicity

❏ stage hand ❏ build/paint sets ❏ make-up

❏ find/make props ❏ costumes ❏ lighting

❏ sound ❏ music/dance ❏ **Patron**

Any previous stage experience?

Name

Telephone

Fax

E-mail

❏ straight role ❏ humorous role ❏ singing role

❏ small role ❏ medium role ❏ large role

❏ stage manager ❏ producer ❏ publicity

❏ stage hand ❏ build/paint sets ❏ make-up

❏ find/make props ❏ costumes ❏ lighting

❏ sound ❏ music/dance ❏ **Patron**

Any previous stage experience?

Name

Telephone

Fax

E-mail

❏ straight role ❏ humorous role ❏ singing role

❏ small role ❏ medium role ❏ large role

❏ stage manager ❏ producer ❏ publicity

❏ stage hand ❏ build/paint sets ❏ make-up

❏ find/make props ❏ costumes ❏ lighting

❏ sound ❏ music/dance ❏ **Patron**

Any previous stage experience?

Planning and organisation forms

Would you like to join us?

The Society is always happy to welcome new members.

Whether you want to perform on stage, help with production or direction, or work backstage, set building, painting scenery, lighting and sound, making costumes or props or whatever please contact us through:

Would you like to help us?

If you would prefer to support us without active involvement, by becoming a patron of the society, please contact:

Help us to help you to help us!

Perhaps you might like simply to advertise in the programme? If so, please get in touch with:

Planning and organisation useful notes for making announcements 1.17

Production casting sheet

Production

Female roles: *Part*	*1st choice + comments*	*2nd choice + comments*	*3rd choice + comments*

Male roles: *Part*	*1st choice + comments*	*2nd choice + comments*	*3rd choice + comments*

Crowds, chorus & child roles	*Who available*	*Who available*	*Who available*

Production cast checklist

Specific comments	Any problem dates?	Given telephone tree	Given rehearsal schedule	Given script	Informed of role	Telephone/fax/e-mail	Name	Role

Production backstage checklist

Job	Name	Telephone/fax/e-mail	Asked to help	Given script	Given rehearsal schedule	Given telephone tree	Any problem dates?	Specific comments

Production notes on rehearsal schedule and groups $\quad$ **2**.5

Dress rehearsals

1
Performance dates are generally fixed so final rehearsals must culminate then. Start your rehearsal schedule at the end and work back from last dress rehearsal date.

2
Try to leave one clear night between last rehearsal and first performance so that everyone can renew their energies before the show begins.

3
Decide how many dress rehearsals are needed – usually a minimum of 2. Aim for 3 full runs in costume, with all the props and scenery changes to establish timing. An early dress rehearsal will spur on the backstage preparations and 'tune up' the cast.

Technical rehearsals
Fix at least 1 technical rehearsal – 2 if possible.

Run-throughs
Have at least 3 run-throughs of the entire play, albeit undressed and unlit, during the last stages of rehearsal. This will help everyone, front and back stage, to have a proper understanding of the continuity and flow and to appreciate how the timing relates to their particular role.

Ordinary rehearsals
Now move back in time, slotting into the diary all the other rehearsal dates. Remember to provide for:

1
Polishing rough areas.

2
Extra time for complicated sections such as fights, sensitive love scenes, and chorus or crowd scenes. Music rehearsals should be dotted throughout to give concentrated attention to singing and choreography.

3
Complete acts: Moving backwards through the diary, plan when to run complete acts. Ensure that time is shared appropriately between acts, balanced to reflect the needs of the play.

4
Introductory rehearsals: Now jump to the beginning of the rehearsal schedule and pop in the first few straight rehearsals with the entire cast to familiarise everyone with the play and allow the plotting of moves.

Note
In a large-cast play, working in teams (depending on which characters interact) in the early rehearsals can avoid some actors having to wait around when the action is 'stop and go back' and 'do it again'. Use the form below to plan this grouping. A major character will, generally, appear in more than one group.

Problem dates
If rehearsal venue is used by other groups, do note any problem dates, such as:
Youth Club: During term time every Friday 6.30 – 9pm.
Women's Circle: 3rd Tuesday in the month

_____

_____

_____

_____

_____

_____

Group A	Group B	Group C	Group D	Group E	Group F

Production planning moves

Play	*Act*	*Scene*	*Script page number*

UP STAGE

WINGS

WINGS

DOWN STAGE
Audience

Blocking the moves in rehearsal

Either:

1
Read the entire play, while blocking in the moves, or . . .

2
Walk through entrances, exits and major moves – but without speaking the lines.

3
Some moves are bound to change. Be open to new ideas.

4
Make sure every actor has a pencil and eraser to note the moves.

5
Try to create an interesting pattern of movement .

Avoid the following:

1
The traffic jam – when too many people approach an exit or entrance at once. Alternate sides. Stagger the moves. Make sure actors are kept clear of entrances and exits about to be used.

2
The crash: orchestrate moves to avoid collision courses.

3
Continuity: Ensure integrity of the world beyond visible stage. Which exit leads to the front door, or garden, for example?

4
Walking through fittings – furniture, walls and scenery are rarely in place at early rehearsals. Establish barriers, entrances and furniture. Use chalk to mark these on the stage.

Try to:

1
Use the entire stage. If rehearsal area is smaller than final stage will be, remember to allow for this.

2
Make the moves look interesting.

3
Keep moves flowing smoothly.

4
Give moves a dramatic value that reflects the situation.

Crowd and choral scenes

1
Do the ground work thoroughly. Work it all out beforehand. Draw up strategic manoeuvres!

2
Move actors as groups: treat the group as you would a single actor.

3
Note any particularly complex routes.

4
Remind actors to keep track of their own movements. The director cannot carry multiple sets in his or her head.

5
Give each actor a number: digits take up less space on your notes .

6
Make sure the moves convey the dramatic essence of the scene – whether a happy bustle or a fearful tiptoeing!

Note
Moves create a link with the dialogue and a stimulus to actors remembering the lines.

Production absentee form

Date   *Who has problems*

It may help to denote special rehearsals or to indicate these by a code:

DR (Dress rehearsal)
MR (Music rehearsal)
RT (Run-through)
TR (Technical rehearsal)

Rehearsal plan may need to be adapted if vital performers in a particular section are unavoidably absent.

Being aware early on will allow schedule to be revised if necessary.

Production glossary of terms and jargon

Areas of the Stage

UR
Up stage right
UC
Up stage centre
UL
Up stage left
R
Centre right
C
Centre stage
L
Centre left
DR
Down stage right
DC
Down stage centre
DL
Down stage left

3D
Three dimensional or creating this effect

A dead
Predetermined position for a flown item

Acting area
The area of the stage in which the actors perform

Adapter or splitter
A means by which two or more electrical devices can be made to share the same power point

Aluminium
Aluminum

Ampere
A measurement of the rate of flow, or current, of an electrical circuit

Apron or extension
Part of the stage projecting into the auditorium in front of the house curtains

Area separation
Dividing the acting area of the stage into suitable units that can be lit independently or together

Auditorium
The audience area beyond the stage

Backcloth
A scenic canvas or 'drop' used across the back of the stage, often serving as a sky-cloth

Backstage
The non-acting area behind the proscenium arch

Bar
Pipe or barrel above the stage for the suspension of lighting and scenery; may be called a batten

Barn doors
Four separately hinged doors on a pivoted frame at the front of Fresnels or PC's. These can be used to shape the beam and prevent spill light Not suitable for profile spots

Batten
Bar from which lighting equipment can hang: also applied to compartment-type lighting or border-lights

Batten
Scenic wood lengths for tautening cloth at top or bottom or timber used to join flats

Boom or light tree
A vertical pipe which can support several luminaires on a number of boom arms.

Border
A horizonatally placed flat or cloth hung from bar or ceiling grid to mask lights and flown scenery from the audience

Box set
A room setting with only three walls

Brace cleat
Attachment on the back of a flat to which the stage brace is hooked

Braces
Supports, usually adjustable, that are fixed to flats. May be screwed to the floor but are mostly secured by weights

Break a leg!
Good luck!

Castor
Caster

Centre
Center

Centre line
A line running through the exact centre of the proscenium arch

Chasing lights
Lights that flash on and off quickly in succession

Cinemoid
Cellulose acetate which is used to make colour filters in the UK

Cleat
Fitting on flats to which throw lines are secured

Cloth
Area of scenic canvas hanging vertically

Colour
Color

Composite gel
Different coloured pieces of colour gel cut to fit together into one colour frame

Control cable
Cable to connect desk to dimmer racks

Costumier
Costumer

Cotton
Cotton wool or cotton balls or a cotton fabric

Cross plugging
A system whereby several luminaires can be made to share the same circuit or dimmer alternately or at different times

Cross-fade
To fade or change from one lighting stage to another

Cue
The moment at which a set, sound or lighting change will be initiated. The cue may be a line in the play, a change of tempo in a song, or a particular piece of action of stage - whatever has been entered on the cue sheet

Cue sheet
A chart on which all the lighting cues of a production are recorded and which the board operator or electrician will use

Curtains
Drapes

Cut cloth
Parts cut away for foliage effect etc.

Cut-out flat
A shaped flat in plywood or hardboard

Cyclorama or sky-cloth
A curved or straight backcloth hung at the rear of the stage. It is sometimes painted white and then lit as required

Darling
Term of false endearment often used by actors; sometimes used to refer to a showy, affected actor

Desk or board
Controller for lighting racks. May also be used when referring to a sound mixer

Dimmer
A device which regulates the power in the circuit feeding a lamp, so as to alter the intensity of the light

Diorama
A scenic view or representation made with a partly translucent painting. If the light shining through it is varied, then the effects change

Down stage
Front half of stage

Drop
Curtain or scenery, usually on rollers, that drops down from above

Dry ice
Frozen carbon dioxide which can be used to produce mist or steam effects

Dying
Forgetting lines and freezing on stage

Earthing
Means by which, for safety reasons, metal parts of electrical equipment may be wired to the ground

Elevation
Scale drawing of a side view of stage or stage unit

Extensions or apron
Part of the stage projecting into the auditorium in front of the house curtains

Eye dropper
Containing stage blood concealed behind a knife blade is used to simulate cutting flesh

Feedback
The sound of the speakers is picked up in the mics and re-amplified. Early signs are a 'colouring' and then that only too familiar whistle! Do not confuse with foldback

Fill light
Light which fills the shadows the key light creates

Fish skin
Fulle setting

Flare
Usually refers to lighting spill, or can be spectral-flare rainbow effects

Flat
Standard unit of scenery with a wooden frame and canvas, plywood or hardboard covering

Flies or grid
The area above the stage where scenery and lighting equipment can be suspended out of sight or 'flown'

Float mics
Microphones arranged across the front of stage

Floats
Area across the front of stage or lanterns used there, often floods

Floats or footlights
A batten of lights set at the front of the stage, which in historical times consisted of floating oil-wicks

Floodlights/floods
Fixed wide angle general spread lighting units, used for illuminating large areas of the stage or cyclorama

Floods
Floodlights giving a wide beam of light, sometimes ellipsoidal reflectors

Floor cloth
Canvas floor covering

Flown
Housed in flies

Fly / Fly mics
Objects / microphones suspended - usually above the stage

Focusing
In theatrical terminology, this does not necessarily mean achieving a sharp focus. Instead it describes organization of the direction, positions, shape, and cover of the beam - as directed on the lighting plan by the lighting designer

FOH
Front of House

Foldback
A signal through speakers or headphones to enable members of the cast, crew, band, etc. to hear whatever sounds that are necessary to enable them to complete their task

Gate
Aperture between the light source and the lens on a profile shutter; may have built-in shutters with which the beam can be shaped, as well as runners which allow for the insertion of an iris or gobo

Gauze or scrim
Large-weave cloth used for scenic effects which can be rendered either transparent or opaque according to the direction and intensity of the lighting

Gelatine/gel
A colour filter medium for lighting, which is made of animal gelatin; it is rarely used nowadays

Gobo (or cookie)
Template of thin metal with cutout design or pattern which can be projected; normally used with profile spotlights

Grid
Wood or metal flats bearing pulley blocks

Ground plan
Scale drawing of a set as seen from above

Ground row
Shaped pieces of standing scenery 60-90cm (2-3 feet) high

Ground-row lighting
Strip light lighting scenery from below; lengths of shallow lighting equipment or battens, for low-level lighting effects

Ham (or hamming it up)
Old-fashioned exaggerated acting (so-called because actors once used ham grease as a make-up base)

Handbag
Purse

Hire company
A rental company

House bar
A permanent flying line

House curtain
The main curtain in a proscenium theatre

House
Everything beyond the stage

House lights
Auditorium lighting

Hum
A sinusoidal signal at a low frequency. Generally assocaited with mains frequency - 50Hz. An unscreened signal lead near to a mains cable or tranformer is frequently the cause

Key light
A light of high intensity, or the most dominant direction of light; the most imortant light on a set which focuses attention, such as moonlight through a window

Lamps
The high-power electric light bulbs used in theatrical lighting equipment

Production glossary of terms and jargon

Left stage or stage left
The area on the left of an actor facing the audience

Leg
Long narrow strip of fabric. Black for masking

Legs
Unframed scenery, canvas wings, or curtains which are hung vertically to mask the sides of the stage

Levels
Rostra, ramps and steps above the main stage

Lighting bar
Lighting or electrics batten, or pipe

Lighting plan or plot
A scale drawing detailing the exact location of each luminaire used in a production and any other pertinent information

Lines
Hemp ropes for raising and lowering scenery

Luminaires
The instruments, lanterns, or units used to light the stage; lighting fixtures

Magazine battens
Border lights or battens which are 'flown' above the stage (UK)

Mains operated
British term meaning electrically powered, using the 'mains' voltage at local or domestic level

Marking
Laying out coloured tape to mark the position of scenery

Masking
To hide certain parts of the stage or equipment or someone from the audience, using scenic devices

Masque
A popular court entertainment in 16th and 17th century Europe, performed by masked players and usually based on a mythological theme. It often included music, dance, and poetry, as well as spectacular effects

Master
A dimmer control (a fader) which controls other submasters, which in turn control the dimmers

Mic
Mike or microphone

Mix
A setting of the controls in sound or lighting

Mock-up
A structural model of the stage and set, often a forerunner to the final detailed model, made to scale

Monitors
Speakers, frequently wedge shaped, used to replay the foldback mixes

Mould
Mold

Neighbour
Neighbor

O.P.
Opposite prompt or 'stage right'

Off stage
Space outside the performance area

On stage
Inside the performace area

OTT
Over the top; exaggerated over acting or overdone staging

P.S.
Prompt side - stage left

Pairing lamps
Joining more than one luminaire to one circuit

Panoramas
A painted cloth which can be wound across the stage to reveal a constantly changing view

Pantomime
English children's fairy tale production put on annually at Chrismas and the New Year

Patching
Using a cross-connect panel which allows any of the stage circuits to use any of the dimmers

Personal prop
A small prop carried on or worn by the actor, such as a handkerchief, spectacles or purse. This is often retained by the actor between scenes, rather than being the responsibility of the props team

Pin hinge
A backflap hinge with a removable pin to act as a pivot. 2 pieces of scenery may be held together using pin hinges. Each half of the hinge is attached to a piece of scenery. A loose pin is inserted through them both. The pivot action of the hinge remains unimpaired

Plot
General list required by all departments noting exact requirements and cues for the entire show

Practical
A lighting fixture or property which is apparently used on the set by the actors during the production, and so is visible to the audience and must be operational. Can also mean any fixture or prop which is illuminated

Preset
A group of faders. Can also mean a pre-arranged lighting state being held in readiness for future use

Profile flat
Alternative to the cut-out flat

Profile spot
Ellipsoidal reflector spotlight; provides a soft or hard-edged beam of light focused by a lens system

Programme
Program

Props / Properties
Anything used on stage (not scenery, wardrobe, light or sound)

Proscenium arch
The stage opening which, in a traditional theatre, separates the actors from the audience: sometimes called the 'fourth wall'

Pyrotechnics
May mean fireworks, but in lighting circles generally refers to any bangs, flashes or smoke that might be required!

Rake
Sloped auditorium or stage to facilitate viewing

Raked stage
A sloping area of stage which is raised at the back (up stage) end

Returns
The number of ways from mixer to stage/amplifiers

Rig
The lighting construction or arrangement of equipment for a particular production

Risers
The vertical part of a step

Roller
Mechanism for hanging canvas cloth

Rostrum
A platform

Roundel
Can mean a coloured glass filter used on striplights. In the historical circumstances, it refers to a small circular window or niche

Run-through or run
Seeing a performance of a play (or one aspect of it, such as lighting) all the way through, from beginning to end

Scissors
An awkward move when two actors cross each other on the stage

SCR
Abbreviation for a silicon-controlled rectifier; a solid state semi-conductor device which operates as a high-speed switch and is used in dimmers

Scrim
See gauze

Set
To prepare the stage for all the scenery and furniture used

Shutters
Part of a luminaire which determines the profile of the beam and can be used to prevent lighting spill on the edges of the stage or set

Sightlines
Imaginary lines drawn from the eyes of the audience to the stage, to determine the limits of stage which will be visible from the auditorium

Sky-cloth
See Cyclorama

Slapstick
Knock-about comedy: the term originates from the wooden bat that clowns or buffoons used to hit others

SM
Stage manager

Specials
Any light which is used for a special purpose or isolated moment in a production rather than being used for general area lighting

Spill light
Unwanted light which spills over its required margins or shows through a gap

Spot bar
Batten or pipe on which spotlights are hung

Stage cloth or drop
A vertical area of painted canvas which can be a backcloth, front cloth, or drop cloth, depending on its position on the stage

Stage left
Left to the actor when facing the audience

Stage right
Right to the actor when facing the audience

Strike the set
Dismantling scenery

Strike
To remove. The opposite of set

Tab
Curtain - front tabs are the main house curtains

Tabs
Stage curtains across proscenium arch

Throw distance
Distance between a luminaire and the area on the stage that it will light

Thrust stage
A stage which is surrounded by the audience on three sides

To fly
To suspend in the air

To focus
To 'set' the lantern directions, beam spread, beam shaping and, with profile spots, the sharpness of the beam edge

To mix
To operate the mixer desk

To plot
To make notes of level setting, cue points, cue times, etc. Applies equally to lighting and sound notes

Tormentors
Masking flats angled up stage and set at the edge of the proscenium

Trap
A door in the stage floor of large theatres, used for special effects and entrances

Traverse
Tabs set on a track across the stage

Trim
Scenery or masking hanging parallel to the stage

Truck or wagon
A mobile platform for scenery

Up stage
Rear half of stage. The area of the stage furthest from the audience

Upstaging
Stealing the scene, often by forcing another actor to turn away from the audience

UV
Ultra Violet. Available in flood and strip versions. Must not be dimmed! At is most effective when used with care and UV paint

Vapour
Vapor

Volt
A unit measurement of electrical pressure between two points in a single circuit

Wagon
See Truck

Washing
Narrow 'pelmet' of curtain that hides the lighting and mechanics above stage

Wing curtains
The soft masking of the wing space

Wings
The area to either side of the acting area or flats at the side of the stage to screen entrances. Actors are often found lurking behind these still 'mugging up' their lines

Wipe track
A single tab track, usually full stage width

Production rehearsal guidelines

First rehearsal

1
It is good to start with the full team gathered, front and backstage.

2
The first rehearsal should establish what is expected of everyone, the style of production and general approach to it. Set goals.

3
Hand out paper matter – schedules, telephone trees etc.

4
Ask members to fill in the absentee form (see 2.9) and any other necessary paperwork.

5
Introduce the music, if appropriate.

6
Provide an opportunity for social mingling; an opportunity for the producer to talk to individuals and ideas to be exchanged.

Play read-through

The first gathering should include a play read-through – or give a summary of the play and its major points, plus the reading of a few excerpts. Make sure the entire plot is understood by everyone before it is segmented up for the rehearsals that will follow next.

Stress the need to:

Attend rehearsals

Turn up on time

Learn lines early

Work together as a team

Hand out any paperwork or schedules not yet distributed: stress that communication is vital. Ensure each member has all the details needed, over and above those on the telephone tree. For example, wardrobe might need information about costume-hire companies.

Throughout all rehearsals:

1
Maximise rehearsal time.
Plan rehearsals well, with approximate timings for when actors need to arrive.

While one scene is being rehearsed on stage, actors not involved can gather in another room, and work through areas that need extra practice.
Keep everybody busy and working hard.

Make sure each section is given appropriate time and commitment.

Be fair.

2
Encourage actors to think! Do not straitjacket the performers. Explore the possibilities together.

3
Stay in control. Discipline is essential. Noise levels must be kept down and members should respect each others' needs.

4
Be aware of potential problems, undercurrents and 'feelings'. Avoid personality clashes.

5
Do not overtire the cast beyond their limits.

6
Keep everybody informed, especially about rehearsal changes.

7
Criticism should be constructive, not destructive.

8
Maintain enthusiasm and be positive. Have the courage of your convictions. Constant stimulation and moving forward will compensate for any extra work imposed on cast and crew.

Line rehearsals

Specific line rehearsals can speed up delivery and reaction to cues. Run through either entire play or whichever sections need concentrated attention. If the prompt can run these rehearsals it will help awareness of 'sticky' patches and improve relationship with actors.

Run-throughs

Complete run-throughs are essential to establish pace, continuity and timing. This will help back and front stage to assess the flow and so be prepared for entrances, cues and curtains.

Stage Management and Props can set stage furniture and hand out any personal props.

Sound and lighting can judge the timing of their effects.

The cast will grasp the flow of entrances and changes.

Technical rehearsals

Thorough technical rehearsal is vital in order to establish the timing of non-acting elements.

Allow time to experiment and to sort out any problems.

Electrics, lighting and other technicalities need sorting prior to the final dress rehearsals, so that these can run smoothly.

If full equipment and/or venue are not available until the last minute, good organisation is even more essential.

A first technical rehearsal does not need all the cast, just the guidance of the producer and a few people willing to stand in the right positions so that lighting angles, special effects, scene and property changes, sound effects, and curtain timing can be tested, adjusted and co-ordinated.

A second 'dry run' might use the actual cast but need only be a quick flash through positions and cues.

Good technical preparation will reduce the inevitable tensions that arise as time runs short.

Production final rehearsals guidelines

Notes for final line-ups

1
The cast must look happy and smile.

2
Individual bows can be taken by actors or pairs of them – or trios.

Ensure:

a continuous flow

that everyone knows the order in which

to step forward

. . . and where to go afterwards.

3
If the actors bow all together, ensure that somebody whom every actor can see is appointed as the lead, so that all bow in unison.

4
Decide if ladies are going to bow or curtsey so that they all do the same.

5
Make sure the orchestra or pianist and lighting/sound teams are given recognition and a chance to bow too.

Curtain calls

Curtain calls must be rehearsed, just like any other element of the performance.

If a musical number is to be performed again as a final flourish, make sure all the cast know the words – some actors may not have performed the chosen number during the show.

The Stage Manager will judge the applause and when to close the curtains finally. The cast must hold their positions and smile until the Stage Manager signals the curtains will stay closed.

Final rehearsals

Technical rehearsal checklist

Have the following been organised?

1
Opening and closing of curtains

2
Clear list of scenes and changes in order

3
Furniture and property positions

4
Entrances and exits for scene shifters and props personnel

5
Timing of fast changes double-checked

6
Normal lighting positions and cues checked

7
Special lighting spots organised

8
Special effects, pyrotechnics and timing of these, especially if several departments have to co-ordinate

9
Sound effects and cues checked

Very last rehearsal

1
Pep talk

2
Run through finale and line-ups (while everyone is there. Children, for example, may have to go home earlier than adults)

3
Run Act One

4
Comments to cast

5
Comments to backstage team

6
Run Act Two

7
Comments to cast

8
Comments to backstage team

9
Run Act Three (if there is one)

10
Comments to cast

11
Comments to backstage team

12
If necessary, re-run any disaster areas

13
Final positive pep talk

Final points to stress to cast and backstage team

1
Don't lurk in the wings and block entrances and exits.

2
Don't chatter or laugh near the stage.

3
Turn up in good time.

4
Consider others.

5
Actors must keep in character until completely out of sight and sound.

6
Maintain pace: cast must be fast on line cues, and on entrances.

7
If something goes wrong, keep the play flowing.

8
Ride audience laughter or fear responses. Actors will need to adjust their timing to accommodate this.

9
Maintain pace. Be prompt on entrances, cues and responses.

10
Remind cast that the Stage Manager is in charge from now on: Responsibility now passes from the Director to the cast and back-stage team.

11
Thank everyone for all their efforts and wish them luck!.

Production guidelines for section 2

2.1
Production: audition form
As well as a vital audition record, this will be a very useful source of information for administration during rehearsals, updating records and for the programme (as a spell check for names and to check if cast use a different stage name).

You will need to know heights when planning pairs, line-ups or chorus groupings.

2.2
Production: casting sheet
Fill in the first choice of cast and adjust as necessary. It helps enormously to see the range of possibilities.

2.3
Production: cast checklist
A useful list of final cast selection and the flow of paper matter handed out. The *Specific comments* column might include details such as:

Could understudy John

Can't arrive on Thursdays until 8.30pm

Moving house 13 May

Wants a singing opportunity, if possible – good voice

2.4
Production: backstage checklist
Similar to 2.4 but for backstage crew when comments might be:

Great at painting, very artistic

Willing to help with sewing costumes

Has back problem – only light lifting allowed!

Unavailable for first dress rehearsal

2.6
Rehearsal schedule
This allows for 32 rehearsal dates. If more than this are needed, copy form as required.

2.7
Special rehearsal schedule
This allows Director to keep track of rehearsals dedicated to special areas: line-learning, music, dance, concentrated children's practice and technical – and to be clear when set construction and painting may involve personnel and the use of the venue.

2.8
Planning moves
To avoid delays and confusion, the main moves need to be plotted in advance of rehearsals, especially if large casts have to be manoeuvred. Of course, some moves will be adapted once actors are on stage.

On a scale drawing of the stage, indicate the furniture, major props and entrances. Characters, represented by coloured pieces of paper, counters or chess pieces can be manipulated until a satisfactory pattern of movement is created. Note entrances and exits and avoid actors crowding, crossing and colliding!

Superimpose these moves onto the stage plans as lines with arrows. Use a different coloured pen for each character and then mark any stationary positions with a circle.

> **See also and make copies from**
>
> **14.3** for alternative stage plans
>
> and
>
> **14.8** for special notes

2.9
Absentee form
In an ideal world everybody needed comes to every rehearsal but this is rarely the scenario! There are bound to be some problem dates. Plan ahead so that rehearsal time is maximised.

Production absentee form **2**.9

Date	Who has problems
January	
Saturday 7	
Sunday 8	John in Germany
Monday 9	John in Germany
Friday 13	
Sunday 15	Susan leaving early (8.45) – David away
Monday 16	
Thursday 19	
Friday 20	
Sunday 22	Chris away
Monday 23	on course
Thursday 26	
Friday 27	
Sunday 29	
Monday 30	
February	Sorry Gill - can't make it till 9pm love Jim
Thursday 2	
Friday 3	
Sunday 5	RUN THROUGH
Monday 6	
Wednesday 7	
Friday 10	
Sunday 12	DRESS REHEARSAL
Monday 13	Pianist late (Sue will stand in)
Thursday 16	RUN THROUGH Prompt unavailable – find someone else!
Friday 17	
Saturday 18	Technical rehearsal
Sunday 19	DRESS REHEARSAL
Monday 20	DRESS REHEARSAL

It may help to denote special rehearsals or to indicate these by a code:	DR (Dress rehearsal) MR (Music rehearsal) RT (Run-through) TR (Technical rehearsal)	Rehearsal plan may need to be adapted if vital performers in a particular section are unavoidably absent.	Being aware early on will allow schedule to be revised if necessary.

Set design plan of campaign

A basic set building kit
Tick box if have sufficient

- ❏ Clamps
- ❏ Cutting and craft knives
- ❏ Drills and bits
- ❏ Glue
- ❏ Hammers
- ❏ Hinges
- ❏ Jars for storage
- ❏ Jigsaw
- ❏ Measuring tape
- ❏ Nails in various sizes
- ❏ Nuts and bolts
- ❏ Pencils
- ❏ Plumb line
- ❏ Right angles
- ❏ Rulers
- ❏ Saws
- ❏ Scissors
- ❏ Screwdrivers
- ❏ Screws
- ❏ Stapling machine

Kit for set painting
Tick box if have sufficient

- ❏ Brushes of various sizes
- ❏ Buckets
- ❏ Masking tape for screening area
- ❏ Newspaper to protect flooring and other surfaces
- ❏ Old margarine tubs or saucers to use as containers
- ❏ Paint
- ❏ Rollers
- ❏ Spoons and stirrers
- ❏ Stepladders

For the next production we need the following

_____

_____

_____

_____

Preparation

1
Assess the overall play and discuss themes with director.

2
Research useful information and illustrative material.

3
Work out a basic structure for the set.

Set team

You will need helpers with practical skills and their own tools to construct the set; and those with artistic skills to help paint the set.

1
Decide how many people are needed to build the sets.

2
Decide how many people are needed to paint the sets.

3
Ask for volunteers.

4
Draw up a rota.

Plan of campaign

1
Plan and present ideas
Give a general overview of how the sets will look and work. Use rough sketches and a scale model to demonstrate ideas.

2
Detailed design
Design individual scenes in detail. Decide on colour schemes.

3
Ordering
Stock check then order any materials and paints required.

4
Set creation
Implement or oversee the structure and painting of the scenery, making sure that the sets work as a whole.

5
Co-ordination checks
Check with the Director and other backstage departments to avoid complications or clashes.

6
Check safety factors
The sets must be practical, safe and take into account fire regulations. Check everything is in working order.

7
Dress rehearsals and performances
Check the sets all work as intended and that the right atmosphere is conveyed. Make any last-minute adjustments.

8
Post performance
Strike the set. Remove everything after the final night and store safely.

Set design guidelines for section 3

3.1

Set design: plan of campaign
Information on planning sets and
construction, plus tick lists for kit needed.

3.2

Set design: stage planning key
These symbols are the standard ones used
when drawing plans of the sets for a
production.

> See also and make copies from
>
> **14.3** Alternative stage plans
>
> **14.5** Stock list sheets
>
> **14.6** Budget sheets
>
> **14.7** Items to be returned
>
> and
>
> **14.8** Special notes

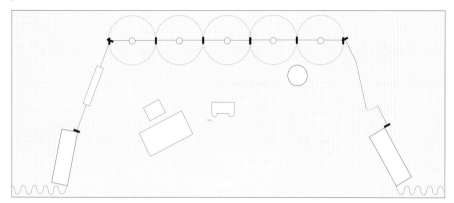

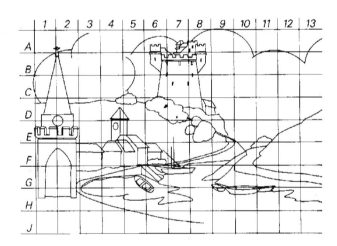

3.3 and 3.4

Set design: grids for scaling – 1 inch
and 1 centimetre
These grids are 10 x 7 inch and 25 x 18 cm.
According to the size of your stage, choose
an appropriate scale, say, 1 inch to 3 feet or
2cm to 1 metre.

A

Measure area to be painted. Do a scale
drawing of design on the inch or
centimetre grid.

B

Provide several copies of the squared-up
design so several people can work at once.

C

Give flats a white coat of paint. When this
is dry, use a chalk line to divide area into
squares. Mark both scale drawings and
flats like a map grid – with numbers along
the top and letters down the sides.

D

Now transfer the designs. First reproduce
a rough outline of the drawing, square by
square, in pencil.

E

Using water-colours or matt household
paint, add the colour to the scenic effect.

3.5

Set design: set building/painting rota
It is very useful to keep track of who has
promised help on which dates and, if play
is moving to a different venue, who can
help transfer scenery.

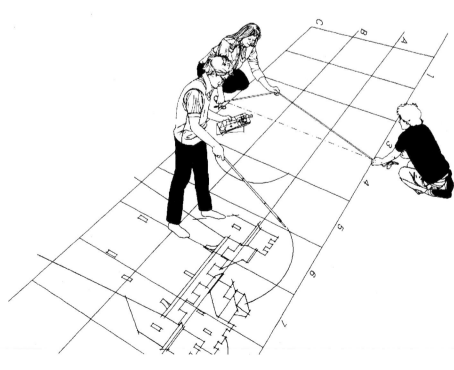

Lighting organising lighting

Aim to:

1
Help visibility.

2
Light actors appropriately.

3
Add dramatic emphasis.

4
Establish time, place, weather and mood.

Aspects to consider

1
Are any specially set lanterns or spots required for this production?

2
Is the current lighting rig able to meet production requirements?

3
Does any new equipment need to be bought or hired?

4
How much power supply is available?

5
Where will the actors be standing in each scene?

6
Which other parts of the stage need to be lit, and how?

7
What is the overall style of the play?

8
Is there any theme or mood which can be helped by the lighting?

9
Should lighting be realistic?

10
Are there any costume or scene colours that will change under the lighting? Are these effects acceptable?

Plan of campaign

1
Assess overall play, discussing this with both producer and set designer.

2
Make a first lighting plan. Plan and present ideas.

3
Research and experiment.

4
Check revised plans with producer and other technical teams.

5
Sort details, work out cues, and make lighting plot.

6
Run through lighting plot until it is very familiar.

7
In rehearsal, check out appropriateness of ideas and incorporate any changes into plot.

8
Stock check. Organise new equipment or hire.

9
Check co-ordination with electricians and any lighting assistants.

10
Make a timetable.

11
Rig lights. Check all angles and focusing.

12
Do safety checks.

13
Technical run-through. Check everything in situ and in sequence.

14
Make adjustments. Alter lights, fixings, angles, and gels, as necessary.

15
Test everything again at dress rehearsals.

16
Man lights during performances.

17
De-rig. If necessary, take down lighting equipment after the show and return or store this safely.

How costume colours change under the lights	Costumes → Lights ↓	Red	Orange	Yellow	Green	Blue	Violet
	Red	Fades and disappears	Becomes lighter	Becomes white	Becomes much darker	Becomes dark grey	Goes black
	Yellow	Remains red	Fades slightly	Fades and disappears	Becomes dark grey	Becomes dark grey	Becomes nearly black
Neutral colours – black, brown and grey – remain almost the same under different lights, apart from a small change in tonal value.	Green	Becomes much darker	Darkens	Darkens	Becomes very pale green	Turns dark green	Becomes nearly black
	Blue	Darkens	Becomes much darker	Turns light mauve	Lightens	Turns pale blue	Turns light mauve
	Violet	Becomes pale red	Lightens	Turns pink	Becomes pale blue	Darkens	Becomes very pale

Lighting guidelines for section 4

Lighting cue sheet

12 During interval make sure moonlight set up ready UC

Act Two Scene 1
The Dining Room 5am.

Curtains are pulled back from the French windows, which are open. Moonlight streams in.

Julia enters down the stairs. She crosses to the window and closes it. She draws the curtains across.

13 low light UR

Then she moves to the drinks cabinet and pours herself a stiff whisky. She opens the door to the hall, listens for a moment and then closes it again. Finally, she relaxes and sits on the sofa.

Enter Roger from the kitchen.

Roger   So this is where you are hiding. Did you really think you'd get away with it? *14 Cut moonlight + bring up 'dawn' lights ready for 15*

Julia   What do you mean - get away with it? Get away with what?

Roger   Oh, Now don't try to be clever with me, young lady. I know exactly what you have been up to. I have been watching you very closely since Saturday night. You're clever, yes. You're devious, oh, yes – and you are also very, very beautiful.

Julia   Cut the crap, Roger. Get to the point.

Roger   Ah, the point! The point! Well, the point is, Julia, my love, that you have committed a very rare crime – a very rare crime indeed.

Julia   And what might that be?

She sips drink, trying to remain cool and collected but her fingers squeeze into the fabric of the sofa.

Roger   You have murdered a dead man!

Julia   (*rising*) Don't be ridiculous!

Roger   (*rising*) No, not ridiculous, not ridiculous at all. Very, very clever, in fact. You have more brains and far more courage than I gave you credit for, Julia. *15 Very low 'dawn' lights UC*

He crosses to window and flings open curtains again.

   Soon it will be dawn, and another day begins – another day as a lonely widow – but this time for real, this time, for the first time, no longer tied to that oh-so-rich but oh-so-boring husband of yours. You are free, my dear, free at last.

He crosses back to her and runs his fingers through her hair and around her neck, menacingly. *Gradually bring up dawn lights during rest of scene*

Cue list

12 UC
Check moonlight OK during interval. Bring moonbeam up just before act starts, as house lights fade.

13 UR
Low light glowing in hall.

14 UR
Cut moonlight as soon as Julia closes curtains.

15 UC
Prepare pre-dawn lights before Roger opens curtains again.

16 UC
Gradually bring up dawn light during rest of scene.

This is the first stage of marking up the script.

Once this has been done, list the cues.

The next stage will be to decide on the specific numbers of lights, their colours and the dimmer calibrations.

Add these details to the Cue List once these decisions have been made.

Uplighting creates eerie shadows

A silhouette effect with high backlighting

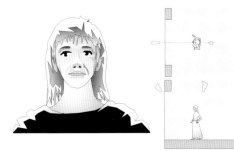

Combine back and front lighting if strong colours are used on the set and the actor is to look normal.

Top lighting is dramatic and highlights the shapes and outlines

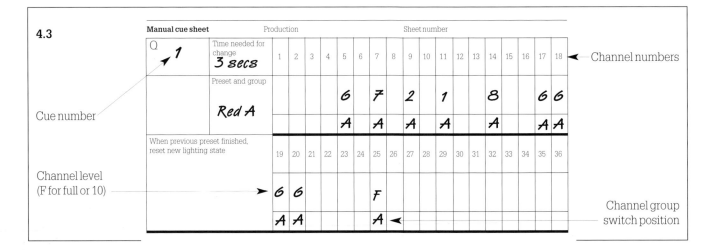

4.3

Cue number

Channel level
(F for full or 10)

Manual cue sheet   Production   Sheet number

Channel numbers

Channel group switch position

Q **1**	Time needed for change **3 secs**	1	2	3	4	5	6	7	8	9	10	11	12	13	14	15	16	17	18
	Preset and group **Red A**						6	7	2	1					8			6	6
								A	A	A	A				A			A	A
	When previous preset finished, reset new lighting state	19	20	21	22	23	24	25	26	27	28	29	30	31	32	33	34	35	36
		6	6					F											
		A	A					A											

Sound aims, plan of campaign and kit

Aims of the sound team:

1

Add dramatic emphasis – such as an explosion or gun shot.

2

Establish 'background' factors such as the sound of surf on a beach, traffic noise, fairground music; wind or drumming rain; birdsong.

3

Supply sounds essential to the plot, such as door bells and telephones ringing, a clock chiming the hour, horses' hooves, news on the radio, a gun shot. These might be taped or mechanical effects

Plan of campaign

1

Read play and highlight when sound effects are needed.

2

Discuss requirements with producer and others implicated (for example, thunder and lightning will need the lighting team). If the play involves musicians, a pianist and drummer can suggest bangs, crashes, tinkling bells and so on, while electric organs offer many background and foreground sound effects.

3

Check what music is needed for pre-performance and during intervals.

4

Make sound plot. All the sound cues and notes will need to be very clearly marked up on a cue sheet.

5

Attend rehearsals. Incorporate any changes or additions into sound plot.

6

Borrow, buy, make or hire any effects or equipment needed.

7

If using taped sound, mix sounds and make up tape with sound effects in correct order. Mark sound plot clearly with the final positions of each sound on the tape. Allow plenty of lead time. Practise during rehearsals to fine-tune the timing and become completely familiar with the routine.

8

Supervise sound effects at dress and technical rehearsals. Make any last adjustments. Finalise co-ordination with stage manager and backstage crew.

9

Be there in good time on performance nights to check everything is in order and to have welcoming music playing in house as audience arrives.

10

After final performance, return any borrowed or hired equipment and store the rest safely.

Basic sound kit
A basic sound kit consists of:

12-way mixer

Amplifier

Pair of speakers plus stands

Cassette deck

Compact disc player

Wheeled flight case for transporting kit

Microphones and stands

Cable, plugs and electrical fitments

For recording in a studio you will also need:

Reel-to-reel tape recorder

Editing kit: a stereo digital recording system is light to carry around, provides good digital sound quality and is simple to use.

Sound effect tapes or CDs:

Sound effects can be created manually or pre-recorded. They can be created specifically or 'bought in' and mixed to suit. They are available from shops and libraries, on record, tape or compact disc. Keep an up-to-date list of all the sound effects you have available and their source. *See 5.2*

Remember...
You will also need a good selection of music for pre- and post-performance Copyright may need to be cleared and permission granted for the group to use the music chosen.

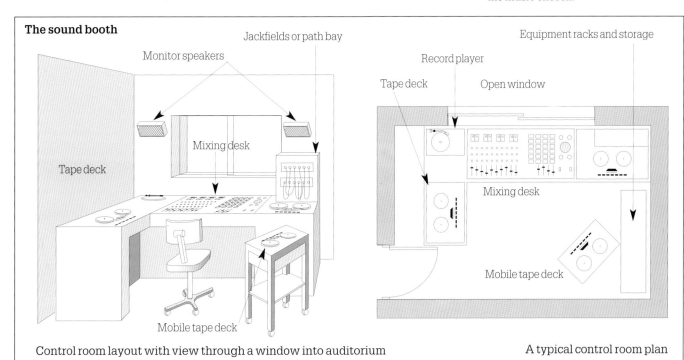

The sound booth

Monitor speakers

Jackfields or path bay

Tape deck

Mixing desk

Mobile tape deck

Record player

Tape deck

Open window

Equipment racks and storage

Mixing desk

Mobile tape deck

Control room layout with view through a window into auditorium

A typical control room plan

Sound guidelines for section 5   **5**.2

Ensure echo microphones plugged in
     ➤ *Fade out 'house' music when S.M. signals*

Scene 1   Mission Control
           Cue sound effect 1 (count-down
            voices, explosion, and rocket take-off)
House Lights fade fast so audience is plunged into a black-out. Curtains remain closed.

Mission Control personnel, in formal poses, all around auditorium, speak in loud thunderous voices.

1   <u>10, 9, 8, 7, 6, 5, 4, 3, 2, 1, ZERO!</u>

Loud explosion and 'take-off' sounds. Brilliant light flashes. Smoke swirls.

Voices
We have lift-off, we have lift-off
And it looks like a good one
Mission Cinderella is on her way; Spaceship Sentaprize is looking good, Sir.
Mission Control wishes to inform The Showman that launch is successful.

The Showman Calling Mission Control. This is the Showman. Congratulations!

Voices   Thank you, sir.
Cinderella is in outer space, Cinderella is in space.
And she's looking good.

Mission Control personnel *on stage relax. Others break through from auditorium and join them.* <u>*Shouts also come from the lighting gantry* .</u> *Remember to shout ! ***

Well done!
Super job!
Sock it to them, Mission Cinderella.
Three cheers for Mission Control! Hip Hip Hooray!
* Hip Hip Hooray!   ➤ *Remember*
Hip Hip Hooray!   *to shout ! ***

Song: Bye Bye Cinders
                   Cue sound effect
                ➤ *2 at end of song*
Scene 2   The Spaceship   *(Computer noises)*

Curtains open to reveal interior of spaceship. All is silent. All is still. In frozen animation, are the Cinderella-Hardup family, encapsulated in 'cocoons'. Slowly wheels start whirring, <u>computers buzz</u>, lights flash on and off.

2 ➤ *The ship is waking. Messages flash across screens, <u>sounds buzz and crackle</u> and entire ship lights up. A screen centre stage sparks into life and reveals the face of **The Showman**, a gauze transformation bringing his face into focus.*

The Showman   This is The Showman calling. This is The Showman calling. May I introduce you to the only creatures still willing to participate in voyages of inter-galactic discovery, to go boldly where no man has been before. Only the most steadfast heroes of fairy tales will man our missions now, zooming into the unknown in frozen animation, to colonize new planets and take the message of true love and happy ever afterings to the rest of the universe.

Sample of a play script marked up with sound effects.

Ensure when you mark up a play script that you mark clearly not only the actual effect but also the moment when you need to prepare the effect in order to be ready in good time.

List of sounds

Blank form for sound personnel to fill in with various effects and sources

It is useful to keep a list of sounds already 'in house' or that you know are readily available, for example on a CD you could buy or from the library

See also and make copies from

14.4 Cue sheet

Sound effects available:

Effect	Have already on (Source)	Know available from (Source)

Music for pre-performance and intervals:

Effect	Have already on (Source)	Know available from (Source)

Props responsibilities and campaign

1

Keep and update a stocklist, showing the items the society owns or can access.

2

Make a full property list for each production, stating exactly what is needed – where when, and by whom. See **6**.2

3

Gather everything in: note who volunteers what. Tick the items as located, delivered or bought – and note down after the show when each item is returned or if it has been added to the society's stock list.

4

Make a plan of property positions on stage.

5

Mark up the play copy with property cues. Allow time to do everything smoothly. *See sample below*

6

Many items will have been borrowed. Props personnel are responsible for the care of these, as well as all the items belonging to the society. Precious items may need to be rescued from actors straight away and put back in the right place so there will be less chance of breakage or loss.

7

Lay out all the properties so that they are ready in good time. A table for each act with the items presented in the right order will help but if space is short, there may need to be a system of rotation.

Factors to consider

1

What is the style and period of the play?

2

Is the property list comprehensive?

3

Does any prop present difficulties?

4

Are there any fast scene changes that must be organised well in advance?

5

The budget: What will the different items cost to procure or make?

6

Is there anything already in stock that is suitable or that can be adapted?

7

Which props are essential to the plot and which ones are optional?

8

Who can help you to make the props?

9

Which pieces might be seen as part of the set design – or require consultation with the set designer?

10

Will anything have to be hired?

Plan of campaign

1

Read play.

2

Discuss ideas with producer and set designer.

3

Research: find information and illustrations.

4

Draw up final lists. Make a plan of on-stage property positions.

5

Mark up script with cues for personal props, props needed in wings and prop changes on sets.

6

Sketch out ideas for anything that has to be made specially.

7

Check through existing properties.

8

Discuss ideas with producer and team.

9

Ask cast and team if they can provide any items or materials.

10

Recruit and instruct any helpers.

11

Buy or make any items needed.

12

Ensure these are approved by producer and/or set designer.

13

Supervise props at dress and technical rehearsals. Check everything looks OK out front.

14

Organise properties throughout performances.

15

After show, gather in everything.

17

Clean, repair and return items as necessary.

18

Update stocklist.

Props cue sheet

Check that:
Table & chairs on marks; bench at 45°
Cutlery set on table
Tray ready in wings
Richard has portmanteau

Act One Scene 3
The Garden

Mrs West and Gertrude are seated at the garden table.
A bench *is stage left.* / Are SETS doing or us?

Susan enters through the rose arbour, *carrying a* tray set for afternoon tea. *She places it on the table.*
+ china, cake, sandwiches

Mrs West Ah, so here is tea, my dear. Will you join me? Thank you, Susan.

Susan bobs a half curtsey and exits.

Gertrude Why, yes; I should be delighted to indulge. It looks delicious. Thank you.

Mrs West Do pour, Gertrude, will you?

For this scene need:
Garden table, 3/4 chairs, rose arbour, bench, tray, tea-set, sandwiches, cake, cutlery, cake knife, portmanteau

Gertrude Of course.

She begins to pour tea.

Susan enters again, followed by Richard. He is carrying a portmanteau. ⸺ Personal prop

Susan Mr Richard, if you please, ma'am.

Gertrude rises as if to make a hasty exit but then recovers and sits again.

Mrs West Richard, darling. What a surprise. And you are just in time for tea.

Richard No thanks, Aunty! Still stuffed from lunch, what ho!

He lounges on bench.
          I say, this weather is just the ticket, don't you think?

Mrs West Quite perfect. Now do tell me all about this exciting scheme of yours. Gertrude has been filling me in but I gather she thinks you are quite mad!

Props property list for show

Prop	Needed by page no. (in script)	Act	Scene	In stock	Buy	Hire	Who making	Set designer organising	Collect from	Who for if personal prop	OS / on stage	Checked and or ready	Cost	Returned

Props stocklist and sources

Furniture	Who has where	Supplier	Owned by society
Lights			
China			
Special items / sundries			
Furniture	Who has where	Supplier	

Props guidelines for section 6

6.2

Property list for a show
This is an (extract) from a typical listing. If the props are numerous, then page 6.2 can be duplicated however many times required.

6.3

Props stocklist
It is useful if a separate record can be kept of the more major items, especially those used most often.

Props property list for show
6.2

Snow White Prop	Needed by page no. (in script)	Act	Scene	In stock	Buy	Hire	Who making	Set designer organising	Collect from	Who for if personal prop	OS / on stage	Checked and or ready	Cost	Returned
PROLOGUE		P											
Sewing kit/needles/fabric	7										✓		
Stools or chairs	7						Ken L				✓		
ACT ONE		1	1										
Chair		1	1								✓		
Small table or dressing table		1	1				Ken L				✓		
Crown jewels,		1		✓						Rob			
Cobwebs	13	1	2				Mary P						
Hand mirror,	13	1	2	✓						Susan			
Duster	14	1	2		✓								
Wooden pail	14	1	2				Bob K				✓		
Velvet spread	18	1	3								✓		
Axe	20						Bob K			Sam			
ACT TWO													
Beds	26	2	1				Chris D				✓		
Handkerchiefs	26	2	1						Mary P	Jenny			
Pots	26	2	1						Mary P		✓		
Warming pans	26	2	1				Simon B				✓		
Cups, plates	30	2	1	✓							✓		

All the small odds and ends can simply be listed in a notepad

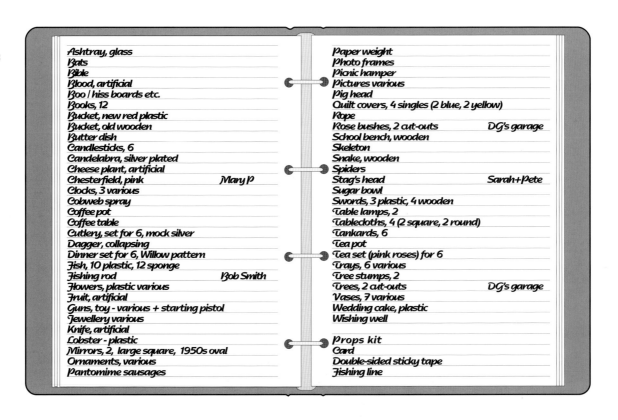

Ashtray, glass
Bats
Bible
Blood, artificial
Boo / hiss boards etc.
Books, 12
Bucket, new red plastic
Bucket, old wooden
Butter dish
Candlesticks, 6
Candelabra, silver plated
Cheese plant, artificial
Chesterfield, pink   Mary P
Clocks, 3 various
Cobweb spray
Coffee pot
Coffee table
Cutlery, set for 6, mock silver
Dagger, collapsing
Dinner set for 6, Willow pattern
Fish, 10 plastic, 12 sponge
Fishing rod   Bob Smith
Flowers, plastic various
Fruit, artificial
Guns, toy - various + starting pistol
Jewellery various
Knife, artificial
Lobster - plastic
Mirrors, 2, large square, 1950s oval
Ornaments, various
Pantomime sausages

Paper weight
Photo frames
Picnic hamper
Pictures various
Pig head
Quilt covers, 4 singles (2 blue, 2 yellow)
Rope
Rose bushes, 2 cut-outs   DG's garage
School bench, wooden
Skeleton
Snake, wooden
Spiders
Stag's head   Sarah+Pete
Sugar bowl
Swords, 3 plastic, 4 wooden
Table lamps, 2
Tablecloths, 4 (2 square, 2 round)
Tankards, 6
Tea pot
Tea set (pink roses) for 6
Trays, 6 various
Tree stumps, 2
Trees, 2 cut-outs   DG's garage
Vases, 7 various
Wedding cake, plastic
Wishing well
Props kit
Card
Double-sided sticky tape
Fishing line

Costumes plan of campaign and kit

First considerations:

1
What is overall style, period, and 'nationality' of the play?

2
How will costumes help to establish character?

3
What colour schemes will be most effective?

4
Is there a strong scenery/set colour to bear in mind?

5
Are there any fast costume changes?

6
What is the budget for costumes?

7
Is there anything already in stock that is suitable or that can be adapted?

8
What features must be incorporated for the purposes of the plot?

Plan of campaign

1
Read play.

2
Discuss ideas with producer.

3
Research information and illustrative reference.

4
Sketch out rough ideas.

5
Check through existing wardrobe.

6
Discuss ideas with producer and rest of team.

7
Buy any materials necessary.

8
Recruit and instruct any helpers.

9
Measure cast.

10
Make (or organise hire of) costumes.

11
Try costumes on cast.

12
Alter as necessary.

13
Work out plan of campaign for quick changes.

14
Supervise costumes at dress rehearsals. Check everything looks OK out front.

15
Be on hand during performances to help with any fast changes.

16
Take a needle, thread, scissors and safety pins ready for any last-minute repairs.

17
After show, gather in everything safely and then clean, repair and return items as necessary.

18
Update stocklist.

Costumes kit

Basic kit

Cutting table

Dress stand

Hanging rail

Iron and ironing board (+ sleeve board)

Notebook and files for measurements and notes

Sewing machine

Storage containers

Zinc bath or bucket for dying

Haberdashery/Notions

Accessories: beads, belts and buckles

Bindings and braid

Buckram

Buttons

Chalk and soft pencils for marking fabric

Elastic in various widths and shirring elastic

Embroidery threads

Hooks and eyes

Needles: heavy, lightweight, embroidery and sewing machine spares

Pins and pin cushions

Press studs

Ribbons

Safety pins

Tapes

Threads: a good variety of colours plus embroidery threads

Zippers

Materials

Clothes from secondhand sources – members of the cast or jumble sales

Curtains: velvet and net are useful

Fabric

Metallic foil

Newspaper, brown paper, tissue or tracing paper for making patterns

Sacking or hessian

Sheets

String and cord

Vilene or other stiffening

Wire – milliner's, fuse wire, garden and galvanised wire

Wool

Tools

Cloths and sponges

Eyelet punch and eyelets

Hat block

Kettle

Measuring tape

Paint brushes

Pinking shears

Pliers

Riveting tool and rivets

Scissors

Stapling machine and staples

Thimble

Utility blades and knives

Yardstick

Other consumables

Adhesives – collect a variety for different uses – including sticking fabric

Colour and metallic sprays

Fabric and leather dyes and paints

Scotch tape and masking tape

Costumes basic patterns

Basic pattern pieces for actors

These basic pattern shapes can be adapted to form many different styles. When they have been fitted to suit the actor concerned, adding darts and gathers will give roundness and more precise fit.

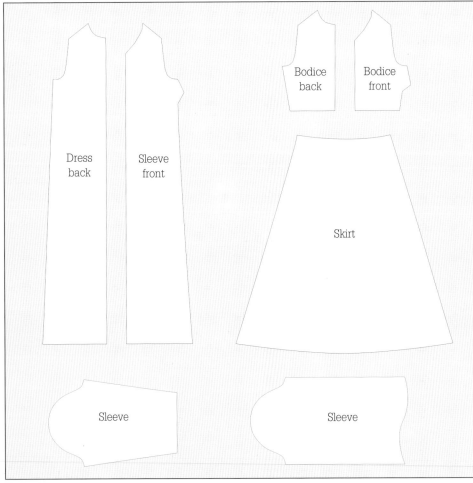

Basic pattern pieces for actresses

Obviously these patterns are the absolute basics, requiring suitable adaptation to create more imaginative styles.

There are many collar and sleeve styles, for example, while the bodice might end anywhere from above the bust to below the hip and the skirt be pencil slim or a 1950s flare.

Costumes cast measurements

Actor / actress + Character(s)	Dress size	Shirt size	Shoesize	Hat size	Circumference of head **a**	Neck to shoulder **b**	Neck (collar size **c**	Armholes **d**	Chest/bust **e**	Underarm to waist **f**	Outer arm-shoulder to wrist **g**	Waist **h**	Waist to ankle **i**	Forehead to nape **j**	Backnape to waist **k**	Centre of shoulder to waist **l**	Shoulder to ground **m**	Hip circumference **n**	Inside leg **o**

Costumes guidelines for section 7   **7**.4

a   Circumference of head

b   Neck to shoulder

c   Neck (collar size)

d   Armholes

e   Chest/bust

f   Underarm to waist

g   Outer arm–shoulder to wrist (with arm bent)

h   Waist

i   Waist to ankle

j   Forehead to nape

k   Backnape to waist

l   Centre of shoulder to waist

m   Shoulder to ground

n   Hip circumference

o   Inside leg

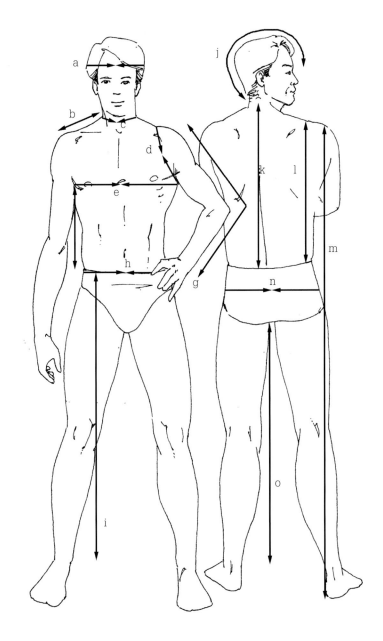

7.1
Plan of campaign and kit
Useful information and listings . The
latter can be ticked off, if required.

7.2
Costumes patterns and cutting out
These basic pattern shapes can be
adapted to create many different styles
– by changing collar and sleeve styles,
skirt widths and bodice lengths. Add
darts and gathers to improve fit on actor.

7.3
Costumes cast measurements
Keep this as a useful permanent record
although, of course, some member's
waistline measurements may change
from one production to another!

7.4
Costumes measurements
Guide to measurements required.
Record measurements on form 7.3

Make-up plan of campaign and kit

The make-up department needs to:

1
Take care of the make-up kit and keep it well stocked.

2
Keep and update a stocklist.

3
Create a 'faces file' that acts as a portrait gallery of make-up done for the group. Include both the rough sketches and the photographs of finished effects – inspiring reference and a source of information for future productions.

4
Make sure a team of helpers is available: work out a rota.

5
During performances, lay out all the make-up to be ready in good time.

Factors to consider

1
What is the style and period of play?

2
How will make-up help to establish character?

3
Does any particular character need research or special attention?

4
Are there any fast scene changes to be organised in advance?

5
Who can help you to do the make-up?

6
Will any wigs have to be hired?

7
What is the budget for make-up in this production?

Plan of campaign

1
Read play.

2
Analyse appearance of characters.

3
Discuss overall style and aims of production and individual characters with producer and the actors concerned.

4
Research background information and how to achieve effects.

5
Make plot of timing, noting any fast changes or when lots of people will need help with their make-up at once.

6
Draw rough sketches of make-up for any special characters.

7
Attend rehearsals to check out ideas and incorporate any changes that occur.

8
Check through stock and buy any new make-up required.

9
Organise hire of wigs.

10
Organise any extra help that may be needed and plan who is doing what and when.

11
Supervise make-up and hair styling at dress rehearsals. Allow ample opportunity to practise difficult or previously untried types of make-up.

12
Check effects out front and make any necessary adjustments. Finalise details and co-ordination with the rest of the make-up team.

13
Be there early on performance nights. Allow plenty of time to make up the masses for any grand opening scenes and to concentrate on complicated characters.

14
Be well organised for any quick changes.

15
After final performance, tidy up and collect everything together, noting any items which need replacement, and returning wigs to hire companies.

16
Update stocklist and faces file.

Make-up kit

Black tooth enamel

Boxes with dividers

Brushes, from fine eyeliner tips to plump rouge mops

Cleansers and skin tonic

Clown white

Cotton (wool) balls and cotton buds

Crêpe for false beards, moustaches, eyebrows and stubble

Eye shadow – powder, cream, liquid and pencil

Eyebrow pencils

Eyeliners – pencil, cake and liquid

Face powder

False eyelashes

False fingernails

False noses of various shapes and sizes

Foundations in various shades: greasepaint, stick, cake or liquid bases

Hair bands, grips and pins

Latex and Derma Wax for special effects such as scars and warts

Lipsticks

Liquid body make-up

Make-up remover and tissues

Mascara

Nose putty

Powder puffs

Rouge

Scissors

Sparkle

Spirit gum

Stage blood

Sticks or pots of lining colours for adding finer detail

Tissues

Towels

Wigs and hairpieces

Make-up chart for women and girls 8.2

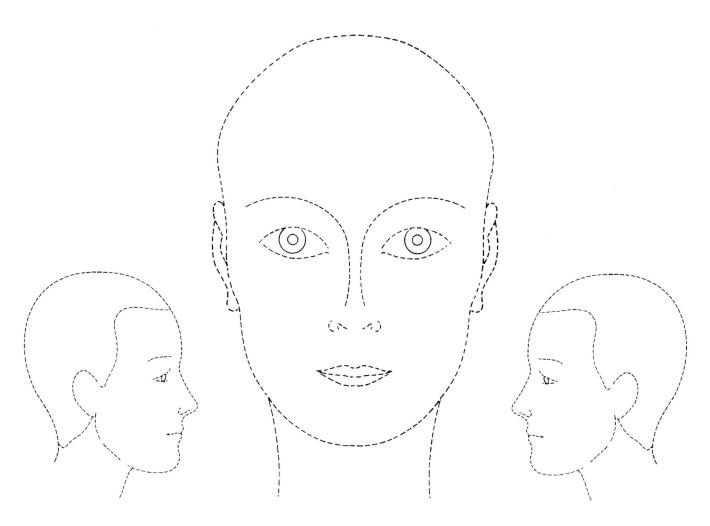

Production _____

Character _____

Actress _____

Base _____

Highlight _____

Shading _____

Powder _____

Moist rouge _____

Dry rouge _____

Lip colour _____

Eye make-up _____

Body make-up _____

Hair _____

_____

_____

Notes _____

Basic appearance _____

Any changes needed _____

_____

_____

Fast change(s) on page(s) _____

_____

Eye make-up needed _____

Special effects notes _____

_____

First appearance on page _____

_____

_____

Make-up chart for men and boys

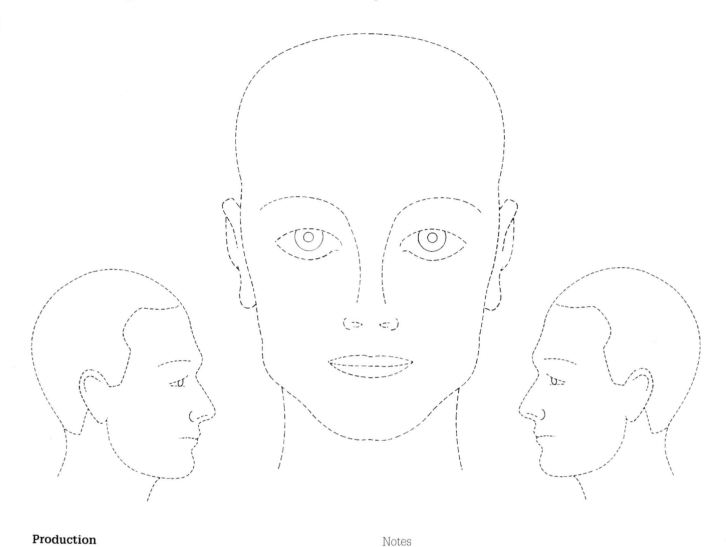

Production _____

Character _____

Actor _____

Base _____

Highlight _____

Shading _____

Powder _____

Moist rouge _____

Dry rouge _____

Lip colour _____

Eye make-up _____

_____

Body make-up _____

Hair _____

_____

_____

Notes _____

Basic appearance _____

_____

Any changes needed _____

_____

_____

Fast change(s) on page(s) _____

_____

_____

Eye make-up needed _____

Special effects notes _____

_____

First appearance on page _____

_____

_____

Stage manager play timing notes

Act / scene / interval		Date	Date	Date	Date	Date	Date	Date	Date	Date	Date
	start										
	finish										
	total										
	start										
	finish										
	total										
	start										
	finish										
	total										
	start										
	finish										
	total										
	start										
	finish										
	total										
	start										
	finish										
	total										
	start										
	finish										
	total										
	start										
	finish										
	total										
	start										
	finish										
	total										
	start										
	finish										
	total										
	start										
	finish										
	total										
	start										
	finish										
	total										
	start										
	finish										
	total										
	start										
	finish										
	total										
	start										
	finish										
	total										
	start										
	finish										
	total										
	start										
	finish										
	total										
	start										
	finish										
	total										
	start										
	finish										
	total										

Total run + interval

Audience gone by

Stage manager checklists

Prior to performances, note

Who is doing what?

Director

Contact numbers

Final set structure

Contact numbers

Props

Contact numbers

Electrics

Contact numbers

Scene shifting

Contact numbers

Lights

Contact numbers

Sound

Contact numbers

Make-up

Contact numbers

Costumes

Contact numbers

Props

Contact numbers

Prompt

Contact numbers

In charge of children

Contact numbers

Security and Emergency

Police

Contact numbers

Fire

Contact numbers

Ambulance

Contact numbers

Theatre manager

Contact numbers

Caretaker/janitor

Contact numbers

Spare keys kept by ?

Contact numbers

Any other

Contact numbers

Contact numbers

Contact numbers

Checklists

The play telephone tree *(see 1.10)* will provide cast telephone numbers, if needed

Prior to curtain up check following ready out front!

Front of House

Musicians

Lighting

Sound*

Prompt *

Any actors entering that way

*may be front or backstage

Backstage check that...

Stage is set for right scene

Props are in correct places

Beginners are made up and ready

Technicians are ready

Special effects are set

Also

Check intercoms, telephones and monitors functioning

Catering in hand

Scene change notes:

Page number

Approximate time

Set change requirements

Which props to set or strike

Any special effects

Actors who need to be ready for next scene

Special requirements

(e.g. fast costume changes)

Any special notes on curtain timing

Stage manager guidelines for section 9   9.4

9.2
Stage manager play timing notes
If there are a large number of scenes, this form can be duplicated as required.

Generally, a performance will speed up considerably from dress rehearsal and first night to the last performance – as these two sample timings show.

Stage manager play timing notes   9.2

Act / scene / interval		Date Feb 11	Date Feb 12	Date Feb 14	Date Feb 15	Date Feb 16	Date Feb 17	Date	Date	Date	Date
1/1	start	7.30					7.35				
	finish	7.51					7.55				
	total	21 mins					20 mins				
1/2	start	7.53					7.56				
	finish	8.19					8.20				
	total	26 mins					24 mins				
1/3	start	8.23					8.23				
	finish	8.44					8.44				
	total	21 mins					21 mins				
Interval	start										
	finish	21 mins					20 mins				
	total										
2/1	start	9.07					9.06				
	finish	9.27					9.25				
	total	20 mins					19 mins				
2/2	start	9.28					9.26				
	finish	9.49					9.46				
	total	21 mins					20 mins				
2/3	start	9.50					9.47				
	finish	10.15					10.11				
	total	25 mins					24 mins				
2/4	start	10.16					10.12				
	finish	10.34					10.29				
	total	18 mins					17 mins				
	start										
	finish										
	total										
Total run + interval		7.30 10.34					7.35 10.29				
Audience gone by		3h 4mins					2h 54mins				

9.3
Stage manager checklist
This will be an invaluable source of information and one copy should be pinned up somewhere where it can be seen readily.

Stage Manager will also need a copy of completed

People needed to organise a production (1.2)

Telephone tree 1.4 or 1.5,

together with stage plans, cue sheets, budget forms and rota of helpers copied from section 14.

Stage manager checklists   9.3

Prior to performances, note

Who is doing what?

Director
Julie Point
Contact numbers
0123 45678
0123 77753

Final set structure
Sam Gold
Contact numbers
1234 67890

Props
Sheila Kirk
Contact numbers
0124 78901

Electrics
Tom Harrison
Contact numbers
0124 91011
0126 78111

Scene shifting
Doug Lane
0123 12345
Contact numbers

Lights
Peter Kirk
Contact numbers
0124 78901

Sound
Tony Black
Contact numbers
0124 123589

Make-up
Cathy Davies
Contact numbers
0124 23456
0126 78910

Costumes
Jackie Tiggs
Contact numbers
0123 91110

Props
Contact numbers

Prompt
Penny Lot
Contact numbers
0123 778899

In charge of children
Joddie Penn
Contact numbers
0123 44455

Security and Emergency

Police
Tattlebury
Contact numbers
0123 99930

Fire
Tattlebury
Contact numbers
0124 90099

Ambulance
Tattlebury
Contact numbers
999

Sheila is a nurse!
Theatre manager
Jim Bane
Contact numbers
0123 33357

Caretaker/janitor
Jim Hold
Contact numbers
0123 00012

Spare keys kept by ?
Sally Hall
Contact numbers
0123 33341

Any other
Contact numbers

Contact numbers

Checklists

The play telephone tree *(see 1.10)* will provide cast telephone numbers, if needed

Prior to curtain up check following ready out front!

Front of House

Musicians

Lighting

Sound*

Prompt *

Any actors entering that way

*may be front or backstage

Backstage check that...

Stage is set for right scene

Props are in correct places

Beginners are made up and ready

Technicians are ready

Special effects are set

Also

Check intercoms, telephones and monitors functioning

Catering in hand

Scene change notes:	Act 1 Scene 2
Page number	23
Approximate time	7.53
Set change requirements	
	Tidy cushions
	Remove rug
	Put chair by 'phone
Which props to set or strike	Strike Tray and note pad
Any special effects	None

Actors who need to be ready for next scene
Tom
Jenny

Special requirements   Check standard lamp on
(e.g. fast costume changes)

Any special notes on curtain timing

Prompt notes

The ideal prompt:

Has a sense of humour.

Is calm, collected and organised.

Has a clear, audible voice.

Can concentrate for long periods.

Is not easily distracted..

Can read small print in semi-gloom.

Can make decisions very quickly.

Knows the play inside out.

Is aware of problem areas in dialogue.

It helps to:

Make an enlarged duplication of the script

Ensure good light in the prompt's corner

Update prompt with any changes or omissions to the script

The prompt is an invaluable aid to line-learning and should attend rehearsals once actors put down scripts. During rehearsals, the prompt should mark the script with comments, vital pauses and 'shaky' areas.

A good prompt is aware of problems immediately and will give the line before the audience notices a gap and the actor is floundering around ad-libbing. Knowing the play well and being able to see the stage and the actors' expressions helps the prompt to discern which pauses are lost lines and which are for dramatic effect.

If actors suddenly jump forward or back in the script, or if a section of dialogue starts to repeat itself, the prompt should guide the actors back to the correct place in the script. Failing this, they must relay a message to the stage manager – a jump forward may mean crucial timing and adjustments.

The prompt copy

The prompt often acts as assistant to the stage manager and is responsible not only for prompting the actors but also for cueing lighting, sound and special effects. To make a 'prompt copy', scale up the script for better legibility and then insert it into a binder, with loose leaves in between. This will allow ample space for notes on all the cues, front and backstage, and for marking in actors' dramatic pauses and shaky areas.

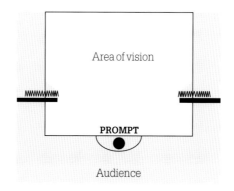

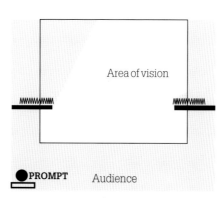

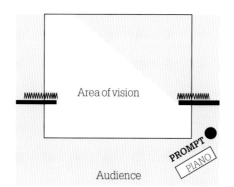

Where should the prompt be?

It is important that the prompt can both see and hear the actors clearly. If a discreet position can be found then hopefully the audience will not be too aware of the presence of the prompt. However, since it is most important that the prompt can see the actors' expressions, do not sacrifice the view of the stage in order to hide the prompt away. If the prompt does end up somewhere very obvious, then dress him or her in suitable costume, if necessary!

Prompt guidelines for section 10

Marking up the prompt copy

The prompt will need a copy of the
script as early as possible in order to
become familiar with the play and to
mark up the pages in good time before
the first rehearsal at which the actors
put down their copies.

Once the play is flowing and all the
actors have put down their scripts,
the prompt should note:

Intended pauses.

Any cuts made to the dialogue.

Any areas where actors have particular
difficulty remembering lines.

---

*Enter three young fellows, Cedric, Fred and
Charles, in striped blazers and boaters.*

Cedric   Oh, I say, you fellows, just come
and look at this view. . .

Fred   Yes, the whole jolly sweep of
Sundown Bay is simply spread out
before us.

Charles   I don't think Cedric's admiring the
landscape. I think he's got his
monocle trained on that spiffing
view just down there.

Fred   Oh . . . oh, you mean–
Keeps forgetting line!

Charles   Yes, the girls!

Cedric   The girls, the girls, my dear chap!
Why do you think we've come
here today? Look at 'em, just look
at 'em!

Slight pause as they gaze out
Charles   All those dinky little knees out for
an airing in the sun!
Fred pauses here /

Fred   Golly!/Well, my Mater always says
that fresh air and exercise stimulate
the appetite!

Cedric   *(laughing)* Ha! Who needs
stimulation, hey what? Wah, wah!

Charles   Wah, wah, wah, wah!

Fred   Wah, wah, wah– But I thought
we'd come here for a little paddle,
chaps ?

Cedric   Well, that's a frightfully sporting
idea, I must say. Let's go and test
the jolly old waters, eh! But hang
the paddle! I vote we go for the full
immersion job. Hey what?

Fred   But it's too bally cold!

Charles   And it's too bally wet! Wah, wah!
Cedric cuts in

Cedric   And it's too bally beautiful to
resist! Just think of it, old sports, all
those delicious darlings down there
disporting in the waves, practically
undressed. Just waiting for us.

Fred   Oh gosh!

Cedric   Look! Take a peek at that redhead
in the clinging stripes.

Charles   *(wolf-whistles)* What a spiffing
little figure.
Pause as Cedric crosses stage

Cedric   *(adjusting monocle)* Not so little,
dear fellow. Those stripes are
shooting all over the place. Corr!!

Fred   Golly! My Mater's warned me
about red-heads.
Pause

Cedric   I say, do be careful, old chap!
You're steaming up my monocle.

Notes on line learning

Play   Scripts supposed to be gone by

Actor or actress	Character	Script down by	Shaky areas

Publicity contact lists and timetable

Local contacts to promote the show

Press

Radio stations

Television

News hand-outs on local activities

Schools and colleges

Charities and organisations

Drama associations and their magazines

Remember:

Voluntary organisations may be glad to bring a group along to the show.
Contact schools and colleges if your play is in examination curriculum.
Promote play in newsletters to members and patrons.

Keep records and update mailing lists.

Encourage members to keep their own personal record of friends, relatives and colleagues who have been before. You might offer a family night with reduced rates for groups.

Other local drama societies may be interested to see your show – especially if you support their plays, too.

Press release information must include:

Name of the group

Title of production

Description of play

Bullet points of show's highlights

Venue

Days, dates and time of performances

Source(s) of tickets

Try to persuade the Press and local radio and television channels to give advance publicity at least one week before – rather than half-way through the production run or after it has finished.

Advance information should include:

Name of the group

Title and author of play

Venue

Dates of performances

Source(s) of tickets

Publicity campaign timetable

Week 1
Prepare Press handouts and newsletters
Check posters, mini-posters and tickets in hand.

Week 2
Contact Press and other promotion outlets.
Post/deliver advance booking forms.

Week 3
Distribute posters, mini-posters and newsletters.
Post/deliver complimentary tickets
Check banner being made

Week 3/4
Organise photography for Press etc.

Week 5/6
Press photographs.
Hang banners.
Update posters with slash banners if necessary.

Contact list form	Contact	Informed	Responded	Contact again
Press				
Radio stations				
Television				
News hand-outs on local activities				
Schools and colleges				
Charities and organisations				
Drama associations and their magazines				

Check the name and address listings on 1.8 and any detailed lists of sponsors, supporters and members for more information on contacts.

Publicity advance information contacts 11.2

Organisation/address	Contact name	Contact numbers	How much notice needed	Comments

Remember to regularly update this contact list. *See also* address book 1.6

Publicity ticket requirements

Tickets

Tickets must include:

Name of the group

Title of show

Day, date and time of performance

Venue details

Concessionary rate if applicable

Row/seat number if applicable

Seat type number if applicable

If you print the tickets on a different colour for each night, this helps when selling and on the door.

Make sure the day of the week and date are clear so that no-one turns up on the wrong night.

A tear-off corner can be used to indicate a child or special category reduction.

Make sure tickets are ready good and early. It is difficult to pin down sales without handing over tickets.

Ticket requirements

Society name

Play

Price adults

Price children

Day	Date	Month	Year
Day	Date	Month	Year
Day	Date	Month	Year
Day	Date	Month	Year
Day	Date	Month	Year
Day	Date	Month	Year
Day	Date	Month	Year
Day	Date	Month	Year
Day	Date	Month	Year
Day	Date	Month	Year

Time

Place

A for adults (cut off for children)

Other information

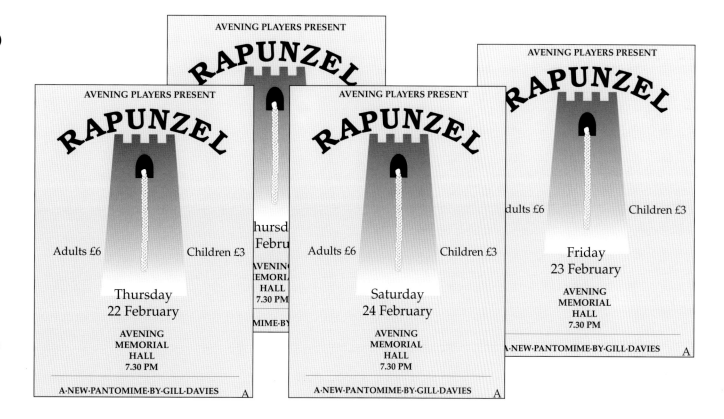

Publicity poster requirements

Posters must include:

Name of the group

Title of production

Author (often a requirement of the granting of license or copyright)

Venue

Days, dates and time of performances

Source(s) of tickets (names, addresses – and contact numbers if possible)

Entrance price and any concessionary reductions available

Posters can be displayed by:

Members and friends of the society

Shops

Libraries

Schools and colleges

Pubs and restaurants

Garages (gas stations)

Village/town halls or equivalent

Sports centres

Mini versions of the poster can be useful for:

A mass distribution

To display on members' car windows

Placing in pub or shop counters for locals to pick up

Mini posters have one big advantage over the poster – the information is taken back into the home.

Poster requirements

Society name

Play

Author

Price adults

Price children

From	Day	Date	Month
To	Day	Date	Month

Time

Place

Other information

AVENING PLAYERS PRESENT

RAPUNZEL

Avening
Memorial Hall
7.30 pm
21 to 24 February

Beer and Wine Bar
every night

Box Office
enquiries
David Moyce
Telephone
0134 567890

Wednesday
21 February
Family Night :
Adults £4
Children £2

Thursday 22
to Saturday 24
February
Adults £6
Children £3
Free supper
included

A·NEW·PANTOMIME·BY·GILL·DAVIES

Publicity programme requirements

Programmes should include:

Name of the group

Title of production and author

Dates of performances

List of acts and scenes

Cast list and backstage credits

Acknowledgements and thanks

A comment on the production by the Director is a useful extra

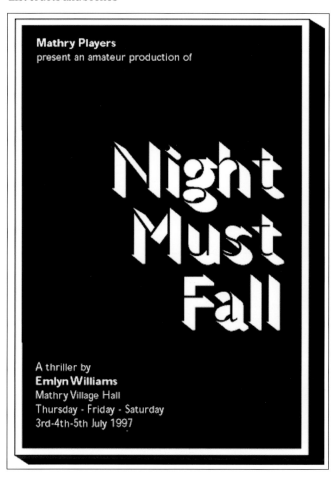

Suggested Programme contents

Page 1
Front cover or title page
Name of the group
Title of production
Author (generally a requirement of the granting of license or copyright)
Venue
Dates of performances, including the year (very useful when archiving!)
Price (optional)

Page 2
Introduction
Optional (often written by the director)

Page 3
The Acts and order of scenes
Interval timings
Any refreshment details

Page 4
Cast list
Usually in order of appearance

Pages 5 and 6
Backstage 'cast list'
This might include the following:
Banners
Box office
Choreography
Costumes
Front of House
Lighting
Make-up
Musical Director
Prompt
Properties
Refreshments
Set construction
Set design
Set painting
Sound
Stage hands
Stage management
Tickets, posters and programmes

Production
The play was directed by . . .

Page 7
Thanks and acknowledgements
It is important to remember everyone and make sure official gratitude is expressed for loan of furniture, seating, sale of tickets and so on

Page 8
End matter
Future productions planned
Invitations to join society or to become patrons
Information about props or costume hire if the company offers these services
Contacts: names and addresses of contacts within the society for future reference

Scattered throughout the programme
Local advertisements: if a small charge is levied for their insertion, this may help to defray costs.
Include the words of songs or carols, if the audience are to join in with these.

Publicity programme formats

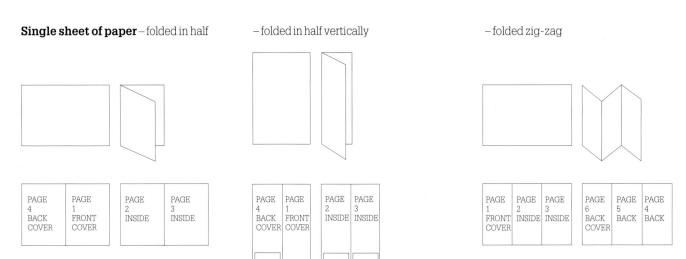

Single sheet of paper – folded in half   – folded in half vertically   – folded zig-zag

A single sheet, folded, is the simplest programme. Vertically folding an A4 297 x 210mm (11.75 x 8.25 ins) or letter size 8.5 x 11 ins (214 x 280mm) sheet makes a programme feel different.

Advertisements can be added to the bottom of the pages.

If adding advertisements, it is easier to keep them all the same size. You can charge more if they are inserted in the front or back cover, but to simplify the design, try to avoid front cover advertising.

If the advertisements raise sufficient money to pay for the printing or photocopying and still provide a profit, you can give the programmes away. This is a good sales point for the advertisers as you can ensure that every member of the audience has a programme – and it is easier to calculate the number required. Do not forget the cast and crew will need a copy each.

Two single sheets of paper – folded in half vertically or horizontally, making 8 pages

| PAGE 8 BACK COVER | PAGE 1 FRONT COVER | PAGE 2 INSIDE | PAGE 7 INSIDE | PAGE 6 INSIDE | PAGE 3 INSIDE | PAGE 4 INSIDE | PAGE 5 INSIDE |

PAGES 2 + 7 ARE PRINTED ON THE BACK OF 8 + 1   PAGES 4 + 5 ARE PRINTED ON THE BACK OF 6 + 3

In the case of an 8-page programme, a little glue to stick in the inside is very neat; with three sheets or more a wire staple is required.

Two single sheets of paper – folded in half vertically or horizontally, making 8 pages

| PAGE 12 BACK COVER | PAGE 1 FRONT COVER | PAGE 2 INSIDE | PAGE 11 INSIDE | PAGE 10 INSIDE | PAGE 3 INSIDE | PAGE 4 INSIDE | PAGE 9 INSIDE | PAGE 8 INSIDE | PAGE 5 INSIDE | PAGE 6 INSIDE | PAGE 7 INSIDE |

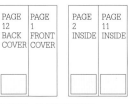

PAGES 2 + 11 ARE PRINTED ON THE BACK OF 12 + 1   PAGES 4 + 9 ARE PRINTED ON THE BACK OF 10 + 3   PAGES 6 + 7 ARE PRINTED ON THE BACK OF 8 + 5

Remember when creating the programme, the odd numbers will always be on the right and the even numbers on the left.

If you wish, the cover can be a heavier paper stock.

Two single sheets of paper – folded in half vertically or horizontally, making 8 pages

PAGE 8 BACK COVER	PAGE 1 FRONT COVER	PAGE 2 INSIDE	PAGE 7 INSIDE	PAGE 6 INSIDE	PAGE 3 INSIDE	PAGE 4 INSIDE	PAGE 5 INSIDE
Next production and/or song	Society Title By-line Place Dates Year	Advertisement / Advertisement / Advertisement	About society Thank you's Why not join us	Back stage team	About the play	Order of acts, scenes and when interval occurs	Cast list
Advertisement		Advertisement	Advertisement	Advertisement	Advertisement	Advertisement	Advertisement

This is a basic guide to the contents, but each play may be treated a little differently.

PAGES 2 + 7 ARE PRINTED ON THE BACK OF 8 + 1   PAGES 4 + 5 ARE PRINTED ON THE BACK OF 6 + 3

Publicity advance booking form

Advance booking form

for:

Dates of performances *

Ticket prices*

I wish to purchase   tickets for the performance on – day   date

Name

Address

Telephone number (daytime)   fax   e-mail

Telephone number (evening)   fax   e-mail

I enclose a cheque for the amount of   Please make cheques payable to *   and send to:

*

(* Insert relevant information prior to despatch)

Advance booking form

for:

Dates of performances *

Ticket prices*

I wish to purchase   tickets for the performance on – day   date

Name

Address

Telephone number (daytime)   fax   e-mail

Telephone number (evening)   fax   e-mail

I enclose a cheque for the amount of   Please make cheques payable to *   and send to:

*

(* Insert relevant information prior to despatch)

Publicity guidelines for section 11   **11**.12

11.1
Contact lists and timetable
The Contact List form may need to be duplicated several times if the society has a large following.

11.2
Make sure Press and media deadlines are inserted clearly on this form.

11.3
Ticket requirements
The Director or Committee should complete this form. It can then be passed onto the person who is designing and creating the tickets – to ensure the correct information is included.

Tear off corners, preprinted with A, can be removed to convert these tickets into concessionary ones – for, say, children or senior citizens – whatever is applicable.

It helps to include the day of the week on the tickets, too, so than any possible confusion is avoided. Otherwise some members of the public may arrive on the wrong night.

11.4
Poster requirements
As with the ticket information, the Director or Committee should complete this form.and pass it along to whoever is designing and creating the posters. The information is slightly different from 11.3 as posters need all the dates and also the contact or box office details for purchasing tickets.

11.5
Programme requirements
Including the year can help when archiving. You might also do this on the poster.

11.6
Programme formats
These are useful suggested guidelines and formats but of course final presentation will depend on the resources and skills available. Individual company's often develop their own individual 'house style' for all their printed matter.

11.6 and 11.7
Advance booking form and Parton/friends form
These are similar but may be sent out at different times, according to the society's policy. Patrons often receive preferential early booking, followed by members' advance booking, followed by the general release to the public.

If there is no accompanying letter, it may be useful to add a 'return by' deadline in the bottom line to ensure pre-booking privileges.

> **See also and make copies from**
>
> **14.6** Budget sheet
> and
> **14.8** Special notes

Advance booking form

for:	*Christmas Crisis*
Dates of performances *	*12, 13, 14 and 15 December*
Ticket prices*	*£5 adults £3 children Wednesday + Thursday £6 adults £4 children Friday and Saturday*
I wish to purchase **4 adult** tickets for the performance on – day **Saturday**	date **15 December**
Name	*John and Sheila Grahams*
Address	*20 Pershore Avenue*
	Minch-on-the Ridge
	Near Tattlebury AB1 3TY
Telephone number (daytime) **0123 37890** fax *same*	e-mail *john&sheilaG@nigriv.net*
Telephone number (evening) **0123 09876** fax **0123 09877**	e-mail *johnG1@aclodge.com*
I enclose a cheque for the amount of **£20** Please make cheques payable to * *Starlight Players*	and send to:

James Monroe — To qualify for privileged advance booking, this form
The Lodge House, Tattlebury Lane — must be returned by *12 November.*
Tattlebury AB3 4TT — And remember, Saturday seats sell fast!

(* Insert relevant information prior to despatch)

11.8
Ticket sales record
Keep these afterwards for future reference. Apart from ensuring correct allocation of seats, the record of ticket sales is useful information when analysing the success of the production, whom to contact again when selling seats, the overall number of tickets sold and which nights sold best.

Publicity archiving photographs and press cuttings   **11**.11

Performance *The Scarlet Wimpernel* Date *March 4, 1992* Photographer or newspaper *Stroud News & Journal*

Around the Valleys

They need seek him no more – he's in Avening!

IT SAYS something for the growing success of the Avening Players that their eighth production – *The Scarlet Wimpernel* – was a complete sell-out.

For four nights the players performed to full houses and those who managed to obtain tickets had a real treat in store.

The play simply rollicked along, with plenty of audience participation, music, laughter and a lively can-can dance from several talented youngsters whose energy left older members in the audience gasping with envy.

The story-line was very loosely based upon *Alice in Wonderland.* Following a little green frog with a white rabbit, Alice crosses the Channel and finds herself in the middle of the French Revolution.

There she meets a delightful melee of characters – dandies and ladies of the court in superb 18th-century dress (Jacquie Biggs, was responsible for some very colourful and impressive

Avening news

costumes), a group of frogs keeping fit at their croakrobics class, and several crazy personalities at the Mad Hatter's tea party.

Ever threatened by Madame La Guillotine – a superb performance by Vivienne Moyce – with her accomplices Madame Defarge and The Executioner, Alice seeks the aid of the Scarlet Wimpernel to help her to escape through the Channel Tunnel back to England. In the event, she took the rest of the cast with her!

The sets were excellent – bright and bold rainbow colours, with a particularly effective Channel Tunnel scene.

The final transformation of Madame La Guillotine into Mrs Thatcher added a delightful twist at the end and was brilliantly enacted by Vivienne Moyce.

Contributed

Churches are blooming and it's thanks t
HILLTOP Gard meeting

⬤ Fabienne Bovis, Sue Werner, Bruce Franklin-Robinson, Gill Davies, Padhi Walker, Jean Franklin-Robinson, Michael O'Kelly and Patrick O'Kelly get into the right frame of mind before another performance of *The Scarlet Wimpernel.* (92-328)

Lib Dems ... er to **Rejection for**

Front of House checklists before and after the show   **12**.1

Before the show

The main job for Front of House is to look after the audience.
However, this means checking the venue thoroughly *before the audience arrives*.

Check tick squares when checked

❑ 1
Check all the house lights, exit lights and emergency lights are working.

❑ 2
Unlock the security chains and bolts from exits.

❑ 3
Check the stage curtain is closed.

❑ 4
Check that auditorium is clean and tidy.

❑ 5
Make sure the float is sufficient.

❑ 6
Prepare any reserved tickets for collection.

❑ 7
Check if there are enough programmes ready to sell.

❑ 8
Put out raffle prizes and tickets.

❑ 9
Put up a sign showing approximate time of final curtain.

❑ 10
Check any information, notices or photograph displays.

❑ 11
Make sure all the seats are set out correctly.

❑ 12
If a cloakroom is provided, are the attendants ready with cloakroom tickets to hand?

❑ 13
Check the toilets and toilet paper stocks

❑ 14
A float may need to be organised. Always make sure there is sufficient change avalable.

Front of House list of responsibilities

Checking seating and seat numbers.

Giving the audience a warm welcome.

Selling tickets and programmes at the door – or overseeing others doing this.

Collecting cash or cheques, and accounting for any monies received.

Dealing with tickets held at the door and allocation of reserved places.

Helping audience to find their places.

Selling raffle tickets.

Ensuring caterers are organised.

Overseeing waiters, waitresses and the bar staff.

Organising any table arrangements, tablecloths or flower arrangements.

Dealing with latecomers.

Coping with emergencies.

Safety considerations

Ensure exits are kept clear in case of fire

Seating arrangements must be in line with safety regulations

All the exit signs must be illuminated

Keep a mobile telephone handy

Cash flow and control

Once all the audience have arrived, the Front of House team will need to 'cash up' and check that the sales figures for the evening are properly recorded.

Each night, separate records should be noted for:

Box office – reserved seat payment

Ticket sales on the door

Meals

Refreshments

Bar

Raffle

Programmes

A final total can then be recorded after the last performance.

Front of House guidelines

1
Be sympathetic, and helpful – but firm.

2
Deal with problems promptly.

3
Try to get everyone seated quickly.

4
Make sure there are sufficient helpers to keep queues to a minimum.

5
Be very polite if problems arise.

After the show

1
Say good-bye to the audience cheerfully.

2
Note any good comments from audience to pass on to all concerned.

Then . . .

❑ 3
Secure the cash.

❑ 4
Tidy up.

❑ 5
Check your notes to see if anything has to be bought or sorted for the next night (e.g., extra raffle tickets or fresh flowers for the tables).

❑ 6
Make sure everything is switched off.

❑ 7
Check there are no taps running.

❑ 8
Check there are no fire risks from abandoned cigarettes.

❑ 9
Fix safety chains, lock up and/or hand over keys.

Box Office

If the theatre has an established box office then all the necessary equipment will probably be in place. If you are starting from scratch, the following will be useful:

Ticket racks or some secure place to hold unsold or reserved tickets

Cash box

Calculator

The up-to-date plan of seating arrangements and tickets sold

Pens, stationery, scissors, stapler and other office essentials

Notebook

Refuse bin

If the society accepts credit cards then, obviously, a credit card machine will also be required.

Front of House bar and food tabs cast and backstage team

Use these forms to keep track of drinks and/or food purchased by the cast or crew during the play run

Name				
Date	Items bought	Price	Number	Total
		Final total due		

Name				
Date	Items bought	Price	Number	Total
		Final total due		

Front of House interval drinks for audience members

If space allows for a separate bar, taking orders for drinks and organising payment in advance can save precious time during the interval.

Upon payment, give the audience member a numbered cloakroom ticket which will allow him or her to trace the right set of drinks.

Then just prior to the interval the drinks can be poured and set out in the bar on trays with the appropriate ticket.

Interval drinks order

Name

Items bought	Price	Number	Total
		Final total due	

Ticket number

Interval drinks order

Name

Items bought	Price	Number	Total
		Final total due	

Ticket number

Interval drinks order

Name

Items bought	Price	Number	Total
		Final total due	

Ticket number

Interval drinks order

Name

Items bought	Price	Number	Total
		Final total due	

Ticket number

Front of house guidelines for section 12 **12**.4

If specific seats are booked, then the Front of House personnel will need copies of completed booking plans – as described in the previous section in 11.9.

12.1
The ticklists and notes here can act as a guideline only. Each theatre and society has a different venue with its own systems and peculiarities! So, in most cases, these Front of House checklists will need to be adapted to suit the particular venue.

12.2
The cast and staff may pay for drinks and food as and when purchased but sometimes, especially for those actors in awkward costumes, – perhaps with only a few precious moments to obtain refreshment – it can be very helpful if they can settle up later. However, always keep a note of those who are not so good at paying up on time or who vanish after the show, to ensure debt collection does not become a problem!

12.4
This system is *fully* workable only if there is somewhere to set out the drinks on trays. A compromise may be needed if space is at a premium, whereby even if the drinks have not actually been poured, the orders have been taken and money has changed hands. This will still save precious moments and reduce queueing time.

Catering
It is vital to ensure that the venue meets all the health regulations and that the food is good, fresh and prepared under hygienic conditions

1
Decide what is to be served or sold and then organise a shopping list for food or refreshments.

2
Decide who is going to buy and deliver the initial supplies.

3
Set up a system for topping up supplies, if this is needed, or to buy any fresh produce daily.

4
Find out if the venue supplies china and cutlery. If so, is there sufficient? Sort out your own, if necessary – or make up any deficit. Everything must be scrupulously clean, of course.

5
If food is being served at tables, these must be prepared beforehand. Clean tablecloths or disposable table 'runners' will be needed.

6
Flowers help the tables look good – a small flowering pot plant on each table may survive better than flowers in a vase.

7
Small night lights on a saucer provide sympathetic lighting on each table but may be against fire regulations. Ask your local fire officer for advice.

8
Remember to buy napkins, refuse sacks, washing-up fluid and any other essentials.

9
Check if you need to bring sponges or tea towels.

10
If ice creams are to be served, access to a refrigerator is an obvious need.

Special notes form, stocklist, rota of helpers & budget form will need to be copied from masters in section 14

Tickets to be collected at the door need to be ready to hand out and easy to find. Keep them in alphabetical order – and if payment is due to be collected, make sure this is clearly stated

Music and choreography music needed

This form can be used by the Musical Director to keep track of music needed for live performance or by the Sound Department to keep a record of recorded music that is played.

Act/scene	Page	Music (Piece/Song title)	From (Symphony/ Musical etc.)	Bought from	(Borrowed from) page/track number	A single piece or album	Copyright cleared*	Returned

Other non-specific songs still needed for

Other non-specific music still needed for

*Sometimes music and lyrics come separately and may have separate copyright.

Cue sheet

Act	Scene	Page number	Cue number	Cue triggered by	Action

Act	Scene	Page number	Cue number	Cue triggered by	Action

Stock list page

This list can be used by any department to keep track of stock and future requirements

Department		Date	In charge	
item	how many	where kept	old/need to replace soon	Running out of

item		source	estimated price	

Hire companies

range	especially good for	contact names and numbers	prices

Can borrow	item	from: names and numbers

At next meeting/rehearsal, put out a plea for

Special notes

Department _____ Name _____

Production _____

Play run dates _____

Date	Note	Action	Comment

Help rota

Department	Name
Production	
Play run dates	

Name	Contact numbers	When available to help	Comment

Reminder notes

To

From   Date

To

From   Date

To

From   Date

To

From   Date

Index

Acknowledgements

Thanks to

VLPS Lighting Services Limited
20-22 Fairway Drive
Greenford
Middlesex UB6 8PW
England
for permission to reproduce their
lighting symbols on page 4.2

Thanks to

A & C Black for encouragement
and good advice

Useful addresses and further reading

UK

Copyright information

The Performing Rights Society Limited
29-33 Berners Street
London W1P 4AA
☎ 020 7580 5544

Fibre optics

Par Opti Projects
Unit 9
The Bell Ind Est
Cunnington St
Chiswick Park
London W4 5EP
☎ 020-8995-5179
Fax 020-8994-1102

Gauzes

JD Macdougall
4 McGrath Road
London E15 4JP

Gobos

DHA Lighting
3 Jonathan St
London SE11 5NH
☎ 020-7582-3600
Fax 020-7582-4779

Blanchard Works
Kangley Bridge Road
Sydenham
London SE26 5AQ
☎ 020-8659-2300
Fax 020-8659-3153

Lasers

Laser Magic
LM House
2 Church Street
Seaford
East Sussex BN25 1HD
☎ 01323-890752
Fax 01323-898311

Strand Lighting Ltd
North Hyde House
North Hyde Wharf
Hayes Road Heston
Middlesex UB2 5NL
☎ 020-8560-3171
Fax 020-8568-2103

Libraries

Drama Association of Wales
The Old Library
Singleton Road, Splott
Cardiff CF24 2ET

Lighting, sound & special effects

Gradav Emporium
613 - 615 Green Lanes
Palmers Green
London N13 4EP
☎ 020-8886-1300

Gradav Hire
Units C6 & C9
Hastingwood Trading Estate
Harbet Road
Edmonton
London N18 3HR
☎ 020-8803-7400
Fax 020-8803-5060

Kave Theatre Services
15 Western Road
Hurstpierpoint
West Sussex BN6 9SU
☎ 01273-835880
Fax 01273-834141

Theatre Projects Consultants
10 Longacre, London,
WC2 E9LN
www.tcpworld.com

Lighting, sound, special effects make-up and staging equipment

Stage Services
Stage House
Prince William Road
Loughborough
Leicestershire
LE11 0GN
☎ 01509-218857
Fax 01509-265730

Machinery

Hall Stage
The Gate Studios
Station Road
Borehamwood
Hertfordshire WD2 1DQ

Triple E Engineering
B3 Tower Bridge
Business Pk
Clements Rd
London SE16 4EF

Unusual Rigging
4 Dalston Gardens
Stanmore
Middlesex HA7 1DA
☎ 020-8206-2733
Fax 020-8206-1432

Paint

Brodie and Middleton Ltd
68 Drury Lane
London WC2B 5SB
☎ 020 7836 3289/3280
Fax 020 7497 8425

Party things

BGS
152c Finchley Road
London NW11 7TH
☎ 020 8201 9222
Fax 020 8201 9111

Projection

AC Lighting
Unit 3
Spearmast Ind Est
Lane End Road
Sands
High Wycombe
Buckinghamshire
HP12 4JG

Optikinetics
38 Cromwell Road
Luton
Bedfordshire LU3 1DN
☎ 01582-411413
Fax 01582-400013

White Light
57 Filmer Road
London SW6 7JF
☎ 0171-731-3291
Fax 0171-371-0806

Pyrotechnics

Jem Pyrotechnics and Special Effects Company
Vale Road Industrial Estates
Boston Road
Spilsby
Lincolnshire PE23 5HE
☎ 01790-754052
Fax 01790-754051

Le Maitre
312 Purley Way
Croydon
Surrey CRO 4XJ
☎ 020-8686-9258
Fax 020-8680-3743

Publications

The Stage
Stage House
47 Bermondsey Street
London SE1 3XT
☎ 020 7403 1818
www.thestage.co.uk

Publishers

Samuel French Limited
52 Fitzroy Street
London W1P 6JR
☎ 020-7387 9373
Fax 020 7387 2161
www.samuelfrench-london.co.uk
theatre@samuelfrench-london.co.uk

Scenery & Fittings

Streeter & Jessel
3 Gasholder Place
The Oval
London SE11 5QR
☎ 020-7793-7070
Fax 020-7793-7373

Signs

Seaton Limited
Department AQ
PO Box 77
Banbury
Oxon OX16 7LS
☎ 0800 585501
Fax 0800 526861

Sound Effects Libraries

ASC Ltd
1 Comet House
Caleva Park
Aldermaston RG7 4QW

Digiffects
Music House (Intl) Ltd
5 Newburgh Street
Soho
London W1V 1LH

Stage Associations

National Operatic & Dramatic Association
NODA House
1 Crestfield Street
London WC1H 8AU
☎ 020-7837-5655
Fax 020-7833-0609

National Drama Festivals Association
Bramleys, Main Street
Shudy Camps
Cambridgeshire CB1 6RA
☎ 01799 584920
fax 01799 584921
TonyBroscomb@compuserve.com

amateur theatre network
AMDRAM
http://www.amdram.co.uk

Stage Make-Up

Charles Fox
22 Tavistock St
London WC2

L. Leicher
202 Terminus Road
Eastbourne
East Sussex BN21 3DF

Theatre Zoo
28 New Row
London WC2

Textiles, paint & make-up

Brodie & Middleton
68 Drury Lane
London WC2B 5SP
☎ 020-7836-3289/80
Fax 020-7497-8425

USA

Blacklights

Wildfire Inc.
11250 Playa Court
Culver City
CA 90230-6150
☎ 310-398-3831
Fax 310-398-3871

China Silk
Horikoshi NY, Inc
55 West 39th Street
New York NY 10018
☎ 212-354-0133

Copyrights

ASCAP
The American Society of Composers, Authors and Publishers
1 Lincoln Plaza
New York
NY 10023
☎ 212 621 6000
www.ascap.com

BMI
Broadcast Music Incorporated
320 W. 57th Street
New York
NY 10019
☎ 212 586 2000
www.bmi.com

SESAC
Society of European Authors and Composers
421 W. 54th Street
New York
NY 10019
☎ 212 586 3450
www.sesac.com

The US Copyright Office website
lcweb.loc.gov/copyright

Fibre Optics

Fiber Optic Systems
2 Railroad Ave
Whitehouse Station
NJ 08889
☎ 201-534-5500
Fax 201-534-2272

Mainlight
PO Box 1352
Boxwood Ind Park
402 Meco Drive
Wilmington DE 19899
☎ 303-998-8017
Fax 302-998-8019

Gobos

Great American Market
826 N Cole Ave
Hollywood CA 90038
☎ 213-461-0200
Fax 213-461-4308

Rosco
36 Bush Ave
Port Chester NY 10573
☎ 914-937-5984
Fax 0181-937-1300

Lasers

Image Engineering
10 Beacon Streer
Somerville
MA 02111143
☎ 617-661-7938
Fax 617-661-9753

Lighting

Strand Lighting Inc
Second Floor
151 West 25th Street
New York NY 10001
☎ 212-242-1042
Fax 212-242-1837

Make-up

Theatrical Supply
256 Sutter Street
San Francisco
California 94102

M Stein Cosmetic Company
430 Broome Street
New York City 10018

Plazma Globes, Crackling Neon
Larry Albright & Ass.
419 Sunset
Venice CA 90291
☎ 310-399-0865
Fax 310-392-9222

Projection

Optikinetics
Rt 1 Box 355B
Doswell VA 23047
☎ 804-227-3550
Fax 804-227-3585

Pyrotechnics

Group One
USA distributors for Jem Pyrotechnics and Jem Smoke Machines
80 Sea Lane
Farmingdale
NY 11735
☎ 516-249-3662
Fax 516-753-1020

Sound Effects Libraries

Gefen Systems
6261 Variel Avenue
- Suite C
Woodland Hills
CA 91367

Dimension Sound Effects
27th Dimension Inc
PO Box 1561
Jupiter
Florida 33468

Strobes, Lighting Effects

Diversitronics
231 Wrightwood
Elemhurst IL 60126
☎ 708-833-4495
Fax 708-833-6355

Jauchem & Meeh
43 Bridge Street
New York NY 11201
☎ 718-875-0140
Fax 718-596-8329

Further reading

Other books in the series

Govier, Jacquie and Davies, Gill
Create Your Own Stage Costumes
A & C Black (UK), 1996
Heinemann. (USA) 1996

Davies, Gill
Create Your Own Stage Effects
A & C Black (UK) 1999
Watson-Guptill (USA) 1999

Young, Douglas
Create Your Own Stage Faces
Bell & Hyman (UK) 1985
Prentice Hall Inc. (USA) 1985

Streader, Tim and Williams, John A
Create Your Own Stage Lighting
A & C Black (UK) 1985
Prentice Hall Inc. (USA) 1985

Davies, Gill
Create Your Own Stage Make-up
A & C Black (UK) 2001
Watson-Guptill (USA) 2001

Davies, Gill
Create Your Own Stage Production
A & C Black (UK) 2000
Watson-Guptill (USA) 2000

Govier, Jacquie
Create Your Own Stage Props
A & C Black (UK) 1984
Prentice Hall Inc. (USA) 1984

Thomas, Terry
Create Your Own Stage Sets
A & C Black (UK) 1985
Prentice Hall Inc. (USA) 1985
Watson Guptill (USA) 1999

For the latest books on drama and theatre contact A & C Black (UK) and Watson-Guptill (Back Stage Books) USA, who publish a wide range of relevant books and will be happy to supply brochures and listings.

Other useful books

Campbell, Drew
Technical Theatre for Nontechnical People
Allworth Press, 1999

Cook, Judith
Back Stage
Harrap Limited, 1987

Davies, Gill
Staging a Pantomime
A & C Black, 1995

Hoggett, Chris
Stage Crafts
A & C Black, 2000

Holt, Michael
Stage Design and Properties
Phaidon Press, 1995

Ingham, Rosemary
The Costume Designer's Handbook
Heinemann, 1992

Ionazzi, Daniel A.
The Stagecraft Handbook
Betterway, 1996

Kidd, Mary T.
Stage Costume Step-By-Step
Betterway, 1996

Jackson, Sheila
Costumes for the Stage
The Herbert Press, 1988

James, Thurston
The Prop Builder's Molding & Casting Handbook
Betterway, 1990

Lebrecht, James and Deena Kaye
Sound and Music for the Theatre
Focal Press, 1999

Lounsbury, W C. and N C. Boulanger
Theatre Backstage from A to Z
University of Washington Press, 2000

Peacock, John
Costume: 1066-1990s
Thames & Hudson, 1994

Peithman, Stephen and Neil Offen
The Stage Directions Guide to Publicity
Heinemann, 1999

Pilbrow, Richard
Stage Lighting
Heinemann, 1999

Reid, Francis
The Staging Handbook
A & C Black, 1995
Design Press, 2000

Reid, Francis
The Stage Lighting Handbook
A & C Black, 1996

Reid, Francis
Designing for the Theatre
A & C Black, 1995

Shelley, Steven Louis
A Practical Guide to Stage Lighting
Focal Press, 1999

Swinfield, Rosemarie
Hair & Wigs for the Stage
Betterway, 1999

Swinfield, Rosemarie
Period Make-up for Stage and Screen
A & C Black, 1997

Swinfield, Rosemarie
Stage Make-up
A & C Black, 1995

Swinfield, Rosemarie
Stage Makeup Step-By-Step
Betterway, 1995

Thudium, Laura
Stage Makeup: The Actor's Complete Step-By-Step Guide
Back Stage Books, 1999